LAKE

The amphibious 1 spread nothing but a of residents in the southwest of Hay Springs, Neb., has made its reappearance, according to a special dispatch to an Omaha paper. Its tactics, which were reported to be unusually menacing in previous cases, were present, causing four motorists to leave their car stalled in a mud puddle, taking to their heels in a desire to escape the reported poisonous fangs.

George Locke of Central City, Neb., Bob Cook of Lakeside, Neb., and two Texas men started to drive overland from Lakeside to Hay Springs. Darkness overtook the quartet and it was decided to stop on the spot as the car had also been stalled in the mire. About 2 o'clock in the morning, Locke declared he was awakened by a commotion in the waters. Looking out from the car, he declares, he saw a fierce and fiery monster, with head and horns sticking clear above the surface of the water. In the dim moonlight, the creature appeared to be of the same size of a small elephant coming in the direction of the car.

Awakening his companions with an unearthly yell, Locke related what he had seen. Almost within the grasp of the monster, the four hurriedly left their car standing in the quagmire, running for their lives. According to the story told by the four, the brute was approximately 100 feet in length.

Look What They Found in Texas

The pigpen of T. W. Tidwell, above, rancher near Dallas, Tex., has become a showplace following his discovery in the ground there of the fossil remains of a prehistoric monster. Dean E. W. Shuler of the school of Geology, Southern Methodist University, has identified the skeleton as that of a plesiosaurus, which roamed Texas some 2,000,000 years ago.

Blytheville Courrier News (February 4, 1931).

COWBOYS &
SAURIANS

IN THE MODERN ERA

John LeMay

Bicep Books
Roswell, NM

First Edition

LeMay, John.
    Cowboys & Saurians in the Modern Era
    1. History. 2. Cryptozoology
    3. Folklore, Early Twentieth Century.

FOR EVERYONE WHO LOVED
THE FIRST BOOK

LIZARD SKELETON REVIVES OLD TALE OF SEA SERPENT

Found in South Dakota; Recalls Lake Campbell "Monster"

BY GLENN MARTZ

Pollock, S. D. (UP)—The recent discovery of the remains of a giant 28-foot marine lizard buried in the shale formation along the Elm River near Frederick, S. D., has revived the story of the "Sea Serpent of Lake Campbell."

Although Prof. James D. Bump, director of the museum at the State School of Mines at Rapid City, says the species became extinct more than 120 million years ago, there are some people in Campbell County who believe one may be still alive and kicking in near-by marshes.

CONTENTS

INTRODUCTION 9

1.	SOUTHWEST RIVER DINOS	19
2.	NEBRASKA'S NESSIE	29
3.	THE FARMER AND THE DINOSAUR	49
4.	BLADENBORO BEAST	57
5.	ATTACK OF THE DINOSAUR MEN	83
6.	TEXAS PTEROSAUR FLAP	89
7.	TYRANNOSAURS ALONG THE TRAIL	113
8.	THE GLACIER MONSTER	123
9.	THE JERSEY DEVIL RIDES OUT	139
10.	THE CARLSBAD CREATURE	157
11.	THE BEAR HYENA	163
12.	THE BUSCO BEAST	171
13.	GIANT SLOTHS OF THE AMERICAS	187
14.	THE MINNESOTA ICE MAN	197
15.	JUNKYARD LIZARD	205
16.	THE SNALLYGASTER	213
17.	GIANT SNAKES OF NEW MEXICO	223
18.	MINI MASTODONS OF WISCONSIN	233
19.	BABY DINOSAUR TRACKS?	239
20.	GOLD AND THE BONES OF A MONSTER	243
21.	A COUPLE CALIFORNIA NESSIES	255
22.	CAVE OF THE THUNDERBIRD	261
23.	THE WHITE RIVER MONSTER	265

POSTSCRIPT:
DEATH VALLEY'S LOST CITY OF THE DINOSAURS 283

APPENDIX 295
INDEX 307
ARTIST CONCEPTS 311
ABOUT THE AUTHOR 312

INTRODUCTION:

CRYPTIDS IN THE 20TH CENTURY

HISTORICALLY SPEAKING, the era of the Wild West came to a close in the year 1895, although others might argue that it extended to and ended around 1912. But however you choose to set its parameters, by 1890, settlement and expansion were definitely coming to a slowing point across the Western United States. The railroad now extended across nearly all of North America, while barbed-wire fences slowly but surely ensnared the once wild ranges and the days of staking claims on unsettled land were coming to an end. As communication lines and telephone poles were erected, the West was no longer as isolated as it once was. Territories like Oklahoma and New Mexico, along with Arizona, became states in 1907 and 1912, respectively. And yet, vestiges of the Wild West still clung to those areas, such as the last stagecoach robbery in Arizona in 1916 and the Mexican Revolution that affected the border states. The Revolution, which stretched from 1910 to 1920, could be considered the last true hurrah of the Wild West.

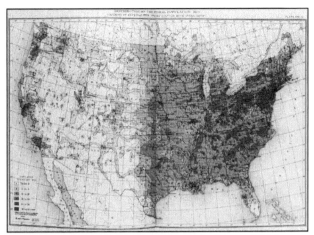

Map of the U.S. Rural Population c.1910.

The "Golden Age of Newspapers" would also see its last hurrah during the decade of the 1920s. There were fewer made-up stories for entertainment, and, for the first time, people could also get their information elsewhere. Radio broadcasts reporting the news began around the year 1920. And, just as newspapers used to occasionally make up stories to entertain readers, radios were now producing audio dramas to the delight of their listeners. However, unlike the newspapers that often passed off fake stories for entertainment as real news, broadcasters were at least straightforward about the fictional nature of their radio plays.

Then, of course, there was the sensational 1938 Halloween broadcast of *War of the Worlds*. Though the performance was preceded by a disclaimer that the audio drama was fiction, some listeners missed the introduction. It also didn't help that the "play" was presented as though it was a series of actual news broadcasts. These "news bulletins" sporadically interrupted the station's normal music programming with reports of strange happenings across the U.S. The "bulletins" told of explosions observed on Mars, followed by a report about an object falling from outer space onto a farm in Grover's Mill, New Jersey. Eventually, reports of widespread panic swept the nation, and though not as catastrophic as some implied, many U.S. citizens were under the impression that a real invasion from Mars was underway.

Special Effects Footage from
The Lost World c.1925.

The War of the Worlds-induced panic was preceded by a similar but less hysteric episode in the form of the release of the 1925 adaptation of *The Lost World*. Before the film's release, or completion for that matter, the author of the book it was based upon, Sir Arthur Conan Doyle, showed a test reel at a meeting of the Society of American Magicians. Among those present was Harry Houdini, and all were astounded at the footage, which featured a family of Triceratops, an Allosaurus, and a Stegosaurus. The film was shown with no explanation for how it was created and as such, some in the audience were left with no other conclusion that perhaps real dinosaurs had been captured on camera. In the words of *The New York Times* the next day, "(Conan Doyle's) monsters of the ancient world, or of the new world which he has discovered in the ether, were extraordinarily lifelike. If fakes, they were masterpieces."

Though it eventually became known that stop-motion animation overseen by Willis O'Brien had created the dinosaurs, there were still plenty of people who thought the dinosaurs were real. And it's no wonder that they did. All throughout the Golden Age of Newspapers, reporters loved to concoct "Snaik Stories,"[1] or tales involving giant reptiles and dinosaur-like creatures of dubious veracity. To this day, it's unknown which of the hundreds of articles present real accounts as opposed to made-up stories for entertainment. The best-known is easily the tale of the 1890

---

[1] Snake was intentionally misspelled as "Snaik" to give readers a hint that the story was either made up, or of an unbelievable nature. Although we know today that some of these "Snaik Stories" were made up, it's also possible that other "Snaik Stories" were real cryptid encounters and were simply labeled as such because they seemed unbelievable.

Tombstone Thunderbird, wherein two ranchers were reported to have shot something similar to a pterodactyl in the Huachuca Desert of Arizona. Supposedly, a photograph of the creature's carcass was taken in Tombstone, and though many people claim to have seen it, said photo has never been located. And, if no photos were ever snapped of these elusive saurians, then we might all well believe that they simply were the creations of ornery newspapermen...

"I was almost on it when a small head turned in my direction and the object, taking fright, made two great bounds, crossed the road and plunged into the loch"

Original Loch Ness Illustration from the *Lincoln Nebraska State Journal* of March 18, 1934.

The idea of prehistoric survivors made a major resurgence in 1934 when the infamous "Surgeon's Photo" was snapped at Loch Ness. One day at the loch, a London gynecologist, Robert Kenneth Wilson, saw a strange, serpentine creature emerge from the waters and managed to snap four photographs of it. Of the four, only one showed a truly clear picture of the creature, and it was sensationally published in the *Daily Mail* on April 21, 1934. Actually, there had been no less than three landmark sightings of the Scotland beastie the previous year, in 1933. But it was the double-whammy of the "Surgeon's Photo" and a sighting by Arthur Grant, who nearly collided with the creature on his motorcycle as it crossed the road, that really set the monster on a path to stardom. Grant's report, published in January of 1934, depicted a near-dead-ringer for a plesiosaurus. The famous "Surgeon's Photo" which followed, of dubious veracity though it may be, all but confirmed a dinosaurian monster's presence in the lake. However, to this day, much like the Tombstone Thunderbird story, the photograph's authenticity is still debated.

At the same time that interest in mystery creatures like Nessie and Bigfoot was beginning to come to the forefront, the world was soon distracted by more pressing matters: the outbreak of World War II. When WWII finally wound down, UFOs became the world's new favorite mystery. And while the late 1940s into the 1950s became the "Golden Age of UFOs", it also marked the birth of cryptozoology thanks to the efforts of zoologists Bernard Heuvelmans and Ivan T. Sanderson.

Heuvelmans published his landmark work *On the Track of Unknown Animals* in 1955, while Sanderson published *Abominable Snowmen: Legend Come to Life* in 1961. The term cryptozoology was coined two years earlier in 1959. Heuvelmans came up with the name, which means "the study of hidden animals" (derived from Ancient Greek *kryptós* meaning "hidden" or "secret."

Bernard Heuvelmans.

With the science of cryptozoology established, the study of this strange phenomenon could finally be cataloged. The 1960s were particularly lively in the realm of cryptozoology with mystery creatures not only being photographed but caught in motion on film. Tim Dinsdale famously captured footage of Nessie just as interest in the creature's existence was beginning to wane in April of 1960. Towards the end of the decade, Roger Patterson and Bob Gimlin caught a sasquatch on camera in Northern California in 1967. Similar to the "Surgeon's Photo" of Nessie, the footage is still hotly contested today with some arguing it's genuine and others certain that it was a hoax.

It would be one thing if all we had to go on was the Patterson-Gimlin footage and the Surgeon's Photo to lend evidence to cryptozoology. But, as it stands, there are many, many other examples of mystery animals captured on film—ones that were far less contested (and perhaps not coincidentally, less famous). There are also far too many witnesses to simply brush off reports of such creatures as nonsense.

Frame 352 from the Patterson-Gimlin Film of October 20, 1967.

And, whereas in the old days, newspaper readers had to take the author's word for it when it came to "Snaik Stories," often with unnamed witnesses in remote corners of the United States, the 20th Century was different. The witnesses appeared not only in print, but on radio and television as well. These were real people. Did they actually see the monster in question?[2] That, as always, was up for debate, but it certainly didn't hurt when they had a photograph to back it up. Or, if not a photograph, it helped when a group of people sighted a strange creature together.

THE MONSTER which prowled the hills of Braxton County on Friday, Sept. 12, was drawn by a New York artist from descriptions given him by Mrs. Kathleen May and Gene Lemon. Flatwoods residents who said they saw the "thing." The two witnesses, with A. Lee Stewart, Jr., Sutton publisher, told their experiences on "We The People" television show in New York Friday night. The artist's conception was featured on the program with a background of weird music. Lemon and Mrs. May hold the portrait which they say is "quite accurate." The photo was taken in Charleston at the Greyhound bus terminal.

A good example is the "Flatwoods Monster" sighted in West Virginia in 1952 by no less than half a dozen witnesses at the same time. Though descriptions of the decidedly alien-sounding creature defied belief, the witnesses all corroborated one another's testimony. As such, despite the alien creature's very odd description, it has emerged as one of the better-pedigreed paranormal cases of the 1950s.

---

[2] Whereas in the old days reporters sometimes made up the strange encounters along with the witnesses that allegedly had them, the people of the modern world quickly learned that they could achieve their "Fifteen Minutes of Fame" by claiming to have seen a monster or a UFO. Thus, the waters were further muddied by attention mongers.

Ultimately, while the 20ᵗʰ Century would end up boasting its fair share of hoaxes and monster sightings of dubious veracity, I still feel that the cryptid accounts of the new century indicated that the "Snaik Stories" of yore had more truth to them than was known. That said, it should be noted that this book will not endeavor to cover every cryptid encounter of the 1900s. Mostly it will cover what I consider to be modern successors to tales recounted in previous entries of this series. For instance, Texas's "Big Bird" flap of the late 1970s presented yet another case of a pterodactyl in the Southwest à la the Tombstone Thunderbird. From that same decade came reports of the Milton Monster in Kentucky, which sounded similar to the Crosswicks Monster reported in Ohio one hundred years earlier. Even the obscure "Dog Eater" of the 1890s had a successor in the form of the better-known Bladenboro Beast of the 1950s. Basically, though set in a more modern era, this volume will focus on the cryptid offspring of the 19ᵗʰ Century covered in previous volumes.

Whether skeptic or believer, I hope you enjoy this armchair investigation into some of North America's more intriguing cryptid encounters of the 20ᵗʰ Century.

SOUTHWEST RIVER DINOS
Compsognathus in Colorado?

A MORE RECENT PHENOMENON in the realm of cryptozoology is that of the Colorado River Dinos—though they are in truth seen across the Four Corners area.[3] One of the more notable sightings happened in 2001 near Cortez, Colorado, when three women driving along a county road saw a bipedal reptile—three feet high and five feet long—dash in front of their car. Because the creature had a long neck and small forelimbs, the creature would seem to match the description of a Compsognathus.

This sighting was discovered via an investigation headed by researcher Ron Scahffer, crypto-zoologist Chad Arment, and Nick Sucik, at the

---

[3] One has even been seen down in Roswell, New Mexico.

time an anthropology student at Northern Arizona University. It all started when Schaffer was contacted over email by an individual known only as Derick, who claimed to regularly see small dinosaurs that were locally called "Prairie Devils." Derick sent Schaffer several modern photos as well as what could be an older photograph. Because it was simply a digital copy, it's unknown just how old the photo is, but it shows a young man (or possibly a young woman) holding up a dead reptile that looks very much like a dinosaur. Even Derick claimed that he didn't know where it was taken or when. Soon contact was lost with the mysterious Derick, and today all we have is the enigmatic photo.

The Famous Photo.

Sucik then made contact with quite a few people in the state of Colorado who had seen the dinosaurs. One of the more notable witnesses was an old-timer named Myrtle Snow. A while back, Snow had read an article debating whether or not dinosaurs were warm or cold-blooded. This prompted her to write to *Rocky Mountain Empire Magazine* in 1982 wherein she told of several incidents in her life involving what appeared to be remnant dinosaurs.

She had her first encounter in 1935 at the age of three when she saw a nest of "five baby dinosaurs" in an outhouse. (Why she considered them dinosaurs rather than lizards is anyone's guess since she didn't seem to offer any significant descriptions.) A few years later, in the late 1930s, something mysterious began killing a local rancher's lambs. In a nearby canyon, the shepherd shot the killer which turned out to be a dinosaur. A Native American ranch hand was tasked with hauling the carcass back to the ranch, which he did using a sled and several mules. "My grandfather took us to see it the next morning," Snow told *Empire*. "It was about seven feet tall, was gray, had a head like a snake, short front legs with claws that resembled chicken feet, large stout back legs and a long tail." In an interview with Sucik, Snow also revealed that the creature was covered in fine grey hairs (similar to the Ceratosaurus of Partridge Creek sighted in the early 20th Century).

Several area farmers came to inspect the creature as it was stored inside a barn. Snow told Sucik that only the Apache youth who had brought it back from the canyon was familiar with the animal and called it a Moon Cow. According to him, they were seen from time to time but were getting rare. Snow claimed the corpse was sent off to a Denver museum (though Sucik could find no record to prove this). Sometime later, Snow sighted a live specimen out in the woods. She claimed she observed it use its forelimbs to grab something from a tree and eat it. She also said the creature's bottom half was hairy and that the top half was green. This wasn't Snow's last dinosaur sighting; she would see it again in 1978, and yet again a bit after her letter was published in the magazine in 1982!

Postcard of Colorado's Dinosaur National Monument.

"I saw another one in a cave in 1937, but it was dark green," Snow explained, then continued that "On October 23, 1978, as I was returning from Chama, New Mexico, about 7:30 P.M., in a driving rain, I saw another one going through the field towards the place where I had seen the one in 1937."

Similar to Snow's story is a rumored episode of *Unsolved Mysteries* which featured two Colorado ranchers coming upon the corpse of a dinosaur-like creature, though no one seems to be able to find it à la the Tombstone Thunderbird photo.

More ancillary evidence emerged from Colorado in 1963, when *The Montezuma Valley Journal* reported in their June 13 issue that "Cortez Museum Scores First with 'Baby Dinosaur' Skeletons". As the headline suggested, two small dinosaur skeletons had been found recently, one in a closed-off mine shaft and the other in a nearby cave. They were taken to the Cortez Museum and curator Ed Roelf tended to think the skeletons belonged to creatures that had died recently as opposed to prehistoric remains. As such, he decided to ask the local Navajo population if they knew anything about these strange, bipedal lizards.

One source identified it as the "hopping lizard," while another called it the "lizard that runs on long legs" in addition to "baby dinosaur." His Navajo informants also told Roelf that the creatures were nocturnal herbivores. Though Roelf thought that the creatures were a modern species of reptile, the newspapers ran with the "Baby Dinosaur" angle and included a picture of Roelf with one of the skeletons in the issue. The photograph featured Roelf with what Nick Sucik described as a "strange dark figure shaped like a small, elongated dinosaur on two legs minus any arms."[4]

Sucik picked up the thread of the missing dinosaur skeletons many years later and trailed them to the Cortez Historical Society. A woman there told Sucik that it was once her job to sort through boxes of unclaimed items from the Cortez Museum when it shut down. Among the items were indeed the baby dinosaur bones, which she sent off to the Denver Museum, which rather quickly identified them as a combination of several mammal bones that had been placed together to resemble a dinosaur. In other words, a hoax.

Colorado River Dinosaur by Neil Riebe.

However, if the bones were actually out-of-place dinosaur bones, would we really expect a government institution to admit it? Any seasoned cryptozoologist or paranormal researcher quickly

---

[4] Sucik, 'Dinosaur' Sightings, *Cryptozoology*, p.156.

learns that the government is more than happy to cover up finds that don't fit the narrative. And while the bones in this case may well be a hoax, the possibility still stands that they might indeed be dinosaur bones swept under the rug. Regardless of the bones' veracity, the Four Corners region is for certain the home to some kind of large mystery lizard that can run in a bipedal stance.

Sources:

Sucik, Nick. "'Dinosaur' Sightings in the United States." *Cryptozoology and the Investigation of Lesser-Known Mystery Animals.* Chad Arment (Ed.). Coachwhip Publications, 2006.

SIDE STORY
PETRIFIED CAVEMAN

Le Moustier by Charles Knight (1920).

The Miami Herald of February 5, 1922, printed this interesting little ditty about a petrified caveman:

Dug out of a coal mine 200 feet below the surface; a strange stone image rests today in the home of Sam Jenkins, a miner living between Welch and Blue Jacket, across the Oklahoma line. Is it the petrified remains of a pre-historic man; the likeness of the first American caveman? Or is it merely a strange freak of nature in molding the human image during the formation of the coal strain?

The image is of black rock. Jenkins digging coal in the end of a drift mine, uncovered it. It is a trifle more than the average human size, showing a deep barrel chest, heavy-muscled arms and legs and a big well rounded head, with flattened forehead and features and powerful wide jaws. The neck is thick and short, the head almost nestling between the huge shoulders. The image is imperfect, for there are no hands or feet.

Before discovering the image, Jenkins, working along the vein of coal, unearthed the footprints of some huge pre-historic animal. The prints were perfectly formed in the shale and were in the same location where remains of a prehistoric animal were unearthed a few years ago. Hundreds of persons have flocked to the miner's cabin to look at the strange image. The image has the appearance of a man squatting, as sitting before a fire.

NEBRASKA'S NESSIE
A Monster of the Roaring Twenties

MOST ALL STATES have at least one lake monster to lay claim to, and Nebraska's most famous water monster once inhabited the depths of Lake Walgren, also known as Alkali Lake. Lake Walgren is a 50-acre body of water in the vicinity of Hay Springs in Sheridan County. Like all lake monsters, witnesses gave the creature a variety of attributes that didn't add up. The most fantastic description made it out to be a kind dragon by way of a giant horned alligator. Others said it looked like a giant catfish, and some a giant mudpuppy the size of a yearling steer. Oh, and there was also a mermaid in the mix once, but we won't get into that here.

Whatever it was, supposedly stories of the monster date back to the time of the Native Americans, but for the most part, the cryptid didn't rear its head in the press until the 1920s.

Postcard of a mudpuppy
c.1950 representing the "monster."

The first article printed on the monster that I could find came from the *Omaha Daily Bee* on August 6, 1921:

Hay Springs, Neb., Aug. 2.—(Special.)—Boy, page St. George, the dragon killer.

Residents in the vicinity of Hay Springs are all "het up" over reports of the discovery of a large sea serpent in the alkali lake six miles southeast of town.

Those who have seen the monster describe it as being about 20 feet long and having a body corresponding in girth to that of a man.

'Tis said the terror can squirt water to a height of 20 feet from its nose or mouth, accompanied by a hissing sound equal to that of a locomotive letting off steam.

It seldom shows itself when anyone is near. For that reason a very poor description of the serpent has been obtained.

Bathers, who hitherto have frequented the lake in large numbers, have lost all desire to enter the water. Intrepid residents are making plans to capture the monster.

On August 16, 1921, the *Alliance Herald* printed an article entitled "Thinks Monster at Hay Springs May be a Whale."

THINKS MONSTER AT HAY SPRINGS MAY BE A WHALE EYE-WITNESS SAYS IT SPOUTED WATER TWENTY FEET.
Mysterious Inhabitant in Alkali Lake Causing Great Speculation Among Residents

There must be something to these tales of a deep sea monster inhabiting one of the alkali lakes near Hay Springs. Reports of some mysterious denizen of the deep have been coming in thick and fast during the past three or four weeks, and finally the Hemingford Ledger has struck an eye-witness who has not only described the fearsome sight, but has permitted himself to be quoted.

The trouble with most of the reports heretofore has been that they have been too indefinite. The Ledger's eye witness gives amazing facts, not only as the dimensions of the monster, but as to his activities. The mystery has been the cause of some outrageous speculations as to the nature of the brute, and up until this last description, the Herald has rather favored the hypothesis that it might be a mermaid. At any rate, read the latest dope on this absorbing mystery. It is but fair to say that the Hemingford Ledger's editor believes the animal is a gray whale, such as are found off the Pacific coast. The Ledger says:

"A more definite description of the large water animal discovered in the Alkali lake is given this week by Arthur Johansen who was in town Friday. Arthur has a quarter section of land lying near the lake and to the west and while at the west end of the lake about 2 p. m. Thursday saw a monster animal lying on the surface of the water and about 300 feet from where he was located. He was first attracted by a warning snort from the horses, and casting about to ascertain if possible the reason, discovered the animal as above stated. Almost immediately after, it emitted a spout of water straight up some 15 or 20 feet which came down in a spray, and then as if having sighted the intruder with a long angling stride it disappeared. "I could see for more than twenty feet the angling waves on the water where it was going," he said.

32

When asked to describe the size and appearance of the animal, said that he did not have time to study the matter but judged that it must be about 10 feet long and 2 or 3 feet broad. It was of a dark grayish color and apparently very active.

"From the description one must conclude that it must be a gray whale which is said to be off the Pacific Coast....

"Following Mr. Johanson's report there were eleven auto loads of sightseers who went out to the lake to investigate, but as a gray whale can only be persuaded to show up with tempting bait and quiet surroundings no one in the party got a glimpse of this much-discussed object."

More articles followed, and one printed on October 21ˢᵗ detailed plans of the game officials to catch the animal. The next year, on August 11, 1922, the *News* ran the headline "The Huge Water Animal Again Seen on Surface." Then the *Omaha World-Herald* ran an article on the monster in 1923 when a witness identified as J. A. Johnson described a forty-foot-long monster. It was a "dull gray/brown" color and had a horn between its eyes and nostrils. For the most part, Johnson and his friends agreed it looked like an alligator. The creature gave a "dreadful roar" upon sighting Johnson and his friends, thrashed its tail, and then dove into the depths.

This was the story that truly set things off and in no time it was picked up as far away as the *London Times.* One of the better-preserved articles came

from the *Nebraska State Journal* on July 14, 1923,
on page two:

STRANGE MONSTER IS SEEN IN NEBRASKA
Four Motorists Stalled Near Hay Springs Are Compelled to Leave Their Car and Beat a Retreat

OMAHA, Neb, July 14—(By the Associated Press) — The amphibious monster, which for years has spread nothing but a genuine horror to the hearts of residents in the vicinity of Big Alkali lake, southwest of Hay Springs, Neb., has made its reappearance, according to a special dispatch to an Omaha paper. Its tactics, which were reported to be unusually menacing in previous cases, were present, causing four motorists to leave their car stalled in a mud puddle, taking to their heels in a desire to escape the reported poisonous fangs.

George Locke of Central City, Neb., Bob Cook of Lakeside, Neb., and two Texas men started to drive overland from Lakeside to Hay Springs. Darkness overtook the quartet and it was decided to stop on the spot as the car had also been stalled in the mire. About 2 o'clock in the morning, Locke declared he was awakened by a commotion in the waters. Looking out from the car, he declares, he saw a fierce and fiery monster, with head and horns sticking clear above the surface of the water. In the dim moonlight, the creature appeared to be of the same size of a small elephant coming in the direction of the car.

Awakening his companions with an unearthly yell, Locke related what he had seen. Almost within the grasp of the monster, the four hurriedly left their car standing in the quagmire, running for their lives. According to the story told by the four, the brute was approximately 100 feet in length.

After their escape, the men returned to the automobile. The car, enveloped in a dense fog coming from the creature's nostrils, they related, was pulled away from the mire only after considerable difficulty and when the monster was absent.

Just what the animal uses for food is the subject of much speculation here. The lake is known to be well stocked with fish and it is possible that its diet may consist of these. Stockmen and farmers in nearby territory of the lake report the occasional loss of a calf.

Next came this piece extracted from the Washington D.C. *Evening Star* of July 25,1923:

GREAT ACTIVE HORNED ALLIGATOR SAYS HUNTER OF LAKE MONSTER.
- Washington D.C.

By the Associated Press.

OMAHA, Neb., July 25. - By far the most vivid picture of actions and appearance of the monster which for about three years has terrified tourists, fishermen, farmers and others in the vicinity of Big Alkali Lake, near Hay Springs, Neb., was received by the Omaha World-Herald today from J.A. Johnson, who signed his residence as Hay Springs:

"I saw the monster myself while with two friends last fall," Johnson's communication stated in describing the monster, "I could name forty other persons who have also seen the brute. But owing to its apparent preference to nights, and apparently dark nights, few have had as good a view as I."

In telling of his experiences, the communication declared:

SEEN IN EARLY MORNING.

"We had camped a short distance from the lake on the night before and all three of us arose early to be ready for the early duck flight. We started to walk around the lake close to the shore, in order to jump any birds, when suddenly, coming around a slight rise in the ground, we came upon this animal, nearly three-fourths out of the shallow water near the shore. We were less than twenty yards from him, and he saw us at the same time we came upon him. It lifted its head and made a peculiar hissing noise and disappeared.

"The animal was probably forty feet long, including the tail and the head, when raised in alarm, as when he saw us. In general appearance the animal was not unlike an alligator, except that the head was stubbier, and there seemed to be a projection that was like a horn between the eyes and nostrils. The animal was built much more heavily throughout than an alligator and was not at all sluggish in its actions. Its color seemed a dull gray or brown, although it was hardly light enough to distinguish color well.

LEFT BAD SMELL.

"There was, however, a very distinctive and somewhat unpleasant odor noticeable for several moments after the beast itself had vanished into the water. We stood for several minutes after the animal had gone, hardly knowing what to do or say, when we noticed, several hundred feet out from the shore, a considerable commotion in the water, like a school of fish sometimes make.

"Sure enough, the animal came to the surface, floated there a moment and then lashed the water with its tail, suddenly dived and we saw no more of him.

"My theory is that there is a subterranean passage from that lake to other underground lakes, and that the beast, and probably others, live underground, coming up only occasionally. Such geological formations are not rare. Many are known to exist in Kentucky and Virginia, where blind fish and other creatures have been frequently found. I can explain nothing more."

37

The Antler's Club, at Alliance, near Hay Springs, yesterday authorized its president to order a whale harpoon, line and whaling gun from a Boston concern, a World-Herald special dispatch stated. A large posse will be formed, and the lake will be thoroughly searched in an effort to find the animal.

One of the original newspaper illustrations.
Nebraska State Historical Society

Our next report comes from the *L'Anse Sentinel* of August 31, 1923:

GREAT SEA MONSTER INFESTS INLAND LAKE.

Omaha. - An order to a Boston firm for a whale harpoon, line and whaling gun was mailed from the town of Alliance, Neb. With it went the interest of thousands of Nebraskans, whose curiosity for years has been piqued by the mysterious freak of Alkali lake, near the village of Hay Springs, Neb.

For two years reports have been originating from farmers that a huge amphibious monster resembling a prehistoric dinosaur has made the alkali water its habitat, coming out at various intervals to prey upon livestock and in some instances terrorizing swimmers, fishermen and autoists who camped nearby.

All doubt in Hay Springs as to the truth of the animal's existence was destroyed two weeks ago, when three tourists appealed to the Hay Springs chamber of commerce to rid the lake of the antediluvian monster, because they had been chased for several yards by the animal.

Two of the tourists were from Texas and the other was a Nebraskan. One of the trio sent in a signed communication to an Omaha paper asking for aid in capturing the freak.

By unanimous vote the Alliance Anglers' club took the first step in ordering weapons. A large posse will be formed, the members announced, and the lake will be searched with the aid of a large drag net. Men with boats will watch the marshy sections with guns and hooks.

After this, it would seem the story fizzled out for a bit until it was briefly mentioned in Mari

Sandoz's 1935 biography of her father, *Old Jules,* which recollected that:

Did Old Jules, pictured above, hear tales of the monster during the Pioneer Period of Nebraska?

Alkali Lake, near Hay Springs, where the early sky pilots dipped their converts, was inhabited by a sea monster – with a head like an oil barrel, shiny black in the moonlight. Some thought it a survival of the coal age. But Johnny Burrows and other fundamentalists of the Flats knew better. The same devil that scattered the fossil bones over the earth to confound those of little faith could plant a sea monster among the sinners. 'Real estate must be moving slow on the Flats,' Jules laughed. When Andy came in, he asked if he had seen anything of the monster. The little grub-line rider took the jew's harp from between his leathery lips. 'No, cain't says I has, but I seen lots o' the stuff them fellahs as sees 'im drinks.'

Though there's not much to this humorous passage, it does at least imply a knowledge of the monster prior to the articles of the 1920s if nothing else.[5] That same decade, in 1938, the monster was dredged up again by the Federal Writers' Project branch in Nebraska, which published an account of the legend in Number Thirteen of their monthly *Tall Tales*:

Since long before the time of Old Jules, a monster sea-serpent has inhabited Alkali (Walgren) Lake a few miles southeast of Hay Springs. He is one of the few inland sea serpents in the world. Sometime down through the years, possibly to distinguish him from

---

[5] However, I should also mention that from what I can tell, Mari Sandoz didn't begin to record her father's biography until the 1920s, when he was still living. As such, Old Jules could have seen articles about the monster and decided to pretend that he had heard of it.

other sea serpents known for their phenomenal performances, he acquired the name of Giganticus Brutervious. So formidable is Giganticus that when he comes to the surface of the water, the earth trembles, and the skies cloud over. Those who have been brave enough and strong enough to endure a glance at him say that his flashing green eyes spit fire, that with a head like a huge oil barrel, he looks like something one sees in a very bad dream, and that the least movement of his big pointed ears causes a tempest on the lake. As he rears and flips his powerful tail, the farmers become seasick for miles around. When he comes ashore to devour his daily ration of a dozen calves, a mist arises so thick that travelers cannot make their way through it, and his flashing eyes color the mist a murky green. The gnashing of his teeth sounds like clap after clap of thunder.

The account went on to tell of plans to capture the creature: "The townspeople estimated the cost of dragging the lake at approximately $1,000. The landowners however asked $4,000 for a three month's lease of the lake and adjacent land, and the Investigation Association would not agree to this price."

For many years, the monster legend rested until it was resurrected again, this time in the January 1962 issue of *Outdoor Nebraska*. On page 24, the magazine wrote:

That Giganticus existed cannot be doubted. There is hardly a fisherman in northwestern Nebraska who will not vouch for the fact, and everyone knows you can always believe a fisherman.

Until the day he died one early-day angler told his tale of seeing Giganticus. While out fishing in Walgren one day, a terrible tempest came over the lake. It then covered about 120 acres. The terrified fisherman tried to reach shore but a combination of tornado and typhoon roared over the water.

More than once he thought he was finished. Just as his small craft plunged over the crest of a wave, he happened to glance down through the water and saw a mountainous peak. It was Giganticus, snoozing. Satan's own had twitched his giant ear and the whole lake became a roaring tempest. Finally, after a day or so, the fisherman fought his way to shore.[6]

As you can see, they listed neither the name or year of the alleged encounter and the magazine was more than happy to promote the sensational story. Likewise, their tongue and cheek resolution to the mystery of the monster's disappearance is rather telling:

Then, an especially intelligent native came up with the idea. If they just ignored Giganticus, maybe he would go away. Hay

---

[6] https://nebraskaland.unl.edu/item/nela.1962_040_01

Springers followed the plan, and no matter what trick the monster tried, it didn't attract any attention. Either bored with life or disgusted that he couldn't create too much of a stir any more, Giganticus stopped making appearances.

Just what did happen to him isn't known. Some think he has gone into some subterranean retreat. Others think that perhaps he has deserted the lake altogether and is now residing in Scotland.[7]

Hay Springs c.1940s.

Supposedly, the last known sighting of the monster was in 1985. However, that is somewhat problematic considering that Hay Springs made a big to do about the monster that same year in the midst of their Centennial Celebration, which used the monster as a mascot of sorts.

---

[7] Ibid.

Furthermore, today good evidence points to the sensational newspaper reports of the 1920s as having been concocted by Nebraska politician and newspaperman John G. Maher. Whether he invented the lake monster articles or not, he did have a hand in several other hoaxes. One was similar to the Cardiff Giant, wherein he buried a cement casting of a Buffalo Soldier at an archeological dig in the vicinity of Chadron to create a petrified man for Nebraska. Yet another involved a mermaid (see side story on page 47).

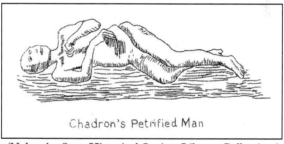

Chadron's Petrified Man

(Nebraska State Historical Society Library Collection.)

More damning information comes from the fact that in 1889/1890, the lake suffered a severe drought that actually turned it into little more than a puddle. How then did the ancient monster seen by the Native Americans resurface thirty years later when it would have had to have relocated in the previous century? So, while there may well have been a monster in the lake's waters back in the days of the Native Americans, the monster of the 1920s was most likely just a fantastic newspaper hoax.

Cartoon poking fun at the monster from the
Lincoln Evening State Journal of August 1, 1923.

Today the village of Hay Springs uses the
saurian for tourism, similar to other "lake monster
towns" across the U.S., selling memorabilia of the
monster in addition to sporting a small recreation
of the creature based upon the 1920s-era
newspaper descriptions.

For a time, there was a brief flirtation with making the monster a mermaid. From the *Lincoln Star* of September 17, 1921:

SAY BIG MONSTER MAY BE MERMAID

Strange Creature in Hay Springs Lake Seen by Mr. and Mrs. Hoefer.

State Game Authorities Plan to Seine the Water — Vicinity Excited.

HAY SPRINGS, Neb., Sept. 17 —
Great excitement prevails in this vicinity over the report that Mr. and Mrs. Charles Hoefer are the latest to get a sight of the sea serpent, mermaid or whatever the monster is, which is said to inhabit one of the lakes near here.

According to the report, it was getting dusk when Mr. and Mrs. Hoefer obtained a sight of the strange creature. It came to the surface of the water, swam around for about 1,000 feet and then went under.

Hoefer said that the portion of the creature that was above water was about the size of a yearling steer and "no one knows how much was beneath the surface."

Great excitement prevails among the female population of this vicinity over the report that the peculiar animal is a mermaid and it is said that many of the wives of the community have forbidden their husband to hunt ducks on this lake.

State game authorities were here about ten days ago investigating reports about the sea monster and stated that they will endeavor to sein it out with a 700-foot seine, as they say it is destructive to the fish.

In 1925, after the furor around the lake monster was dying down, the mermaid idea was resuscitated via this telegram from the *Omaha World-Herald*: "Have a tip that Bruce Heweitt and J. Mayes of Rushville solved the Hay Springs Lake mystery by finding a mermaid frozen in ice of the lake. Wire 300 word story if above is correct, also rush photo of mermaid."

THE FARMER
AND THE DINOSAUR
Why Did the Dinosaur Cross the Road?

YOU'VE BEEN ASKED many times why the chicken crossed the road, but what about the dinosaur? Near Lake Campbell in South Dakota, a farmer driving a tractor down a rural road had to swerve to avoid what he called a dinosaur crossing the road. The description would seem to match that of a theropod or plesiosaur of some kind and the event took place in 1934. Unfortunately, I was unable to dig up the original article, but I did find this follow-up article of sorts from 1946 that recalls the tale:

LIZARD SKELETON REVIVES OLD
TALE OF SEA SERPENT
Found in South Dakota; Recalls Lake
Campbell "Monster"

Dinosaur Park, Rapid City, South Dakota
(Library of Congress).

Pollock, S.D. (AP)— The recent discovery of the remains of a giant 28 foot marine lizard buried in the shale formation along the East River near Frederick S.D. has revived the story of the "Sea Serpent of Lake Campbell."

Although Prof. James D. Bump, director of the museum at the state school of mines at Rapid City, says the species became extinct more than 120 million years ago, there are some people in Campbell County who believe one may be still alive and kicking in nearby marshes.

They recall the strange story of a farmer about 12 years ago who told how he was forced to take the ditch with his tractor to avoid running down a giant four legged serpentine monster which slithered across the road.

Find Tracks to Lake

A skeptical townspeople became suddenly mute when they were taken to the scene and tracked the creature across a muddy field where it had wormed its way into the deep waters of Lake Campbell.

Periodic reports of seeing its tracks and the reported loss of many young pigs and lands strengthen the story.

In recent years it was all but forgotten – until the recent find about 50 miles east.

Technically known as a mosasaur, the lizard skeleton was found by a Frederick high school youth—Don Neff—who did some sleuthing after he discovered the reptiles teeth among some tables he had scooped up from the waters of the stream.

Rare Specimen

Prof. Bump, who was authorized by Brown County authorities to excavate and take possession of the find, is now supervising the delicate job of mounting it for public exhibition at the school of mines.

He estimates the skeleton has lain in that script for several million years and says it is one of the rarest specimens of its kind ever uncovered in the Northwest.

Meanwhile, the eyes of Campbell County residents are scanning Lake Campbell for a glimpse of the real McCoy.

They are curious to determine whether the creature believed seen a dozen years ago is a figment of the imagination or the lone survivor of a prehistoric age.

It should be noted that the same year that the Lake Campbell farmer saw the dinosaur, Loch Ness was making major waves in the news and Nessie sightings had begun to get worldwide attention starting in 1933. By 1934, Nessie was a sensation thanks to the controversial "Surgeon's Photo" taken in April. One has to wonder if the farmer was inspired to make up a serpent sighting due to Nessie's popularity that year. For instance, there was even a similar story about a man, Arthur Grant, almost hitting Nessie with his motorcycle along a lonely road in January of 1934.

Fred's Certain It Looked Like Huge Dinosaur

POCATELLO, Idaho, Oct. 25 (U.P.)—Perhaps it's catching, but Fred Rouse stood firm today on his sober conviction that he saw a "strange looking animal" in American Falls lake.

Strange tales of similar sea beasts have been reported from coast cities, but Rouse's was the first here.

"Recently I was standing on the southeast bank of the American Falls lake," he said. "The water was a turbulent sea of leaden gray rollers from a strong wind. Then I could scarcely believe my eyes for only a short distance from the shore was some large animal moving about."

The creature, he explained, was reminiscent of a huge dinosaur.

"The mouth was fully two feet from snout to jaw. I saw it open, revealing clean shining teeth as it fed in the shallow water."

Stunned with fear and surprise, Rouse said he stood motionless for several minutes until finally the creature swam toward the west end of the lake. It made a sucking, swishing noise as it went.

Story from around the same time in the *Twin Falls Idaho Evening Times* of October 25, 1933.

The famous Loch Ness "Surgeon's Photo" of 1934 which kicked off a great deal of interest in lake monsters in general.

Unfortunately, because the article lists no names, there's no way to research the farmer who saw the Lake Campbell Monster. On the other hand, the article implies that pigs really were going missing at the time that the tracks were found—though the tracks could have been man-made. Furthermore, the monster was a one-off so far as myself and other researchers can tell. Nor is there a regularly seen "serpent" in the depths of Lake Campbell. Or, if there is, no one has been reporting it.

SIDE STORY

Rather routine lake monster story from the *Janesville Daily Gazette* of August 22, 1910:

"Waupaca County's Sea Serpent Story"
Strange "Beastie" That Crawls or Swims, With Huge Paws And Frightens People

Clintonville, WI- Waupaca County and its Clover Leaf Lakes have a sea serpent story. Eight reputable residents have seen the monster. As a result, terror reigns among the Milwaukee and Chicago people who have cottages along the lakes. As described by those who have seen the thing, it is more than six feet long, can swim on the surface or crawl about on the bottom. Its feet have long claws. Last Thursday it chased two women in a boat. William A. Schrander, the city treasurer of Clintonville, has seen the thing also. A baby alligator was turned loose in the lakes some years ago and the supposed sea serpent may be this reptile.

BLADENBORO POLICE CHIEF ROY FORES examine one of the victims of the mysterious 'vampire beast' which has terrorized citizens of that area. Tentatively identified as a huge cat that is a blood sucker, the beast has slain over seven dogs and last night attacked its first human. The beast fled, however, before inflicting any injury. The Bladenboro officer holds up the head of one of the dogs killed by the mysterious marauder. (game photo)

BLADENBORO BEAST
Return of the Dog Eater

BUCKLE UP, because this is going to be a long one. In book two of this series, *Cowboys & Saurians: Ice Age*, I covered a notorious cryptid collectively known as the Dog Eater. The mystery animal was the scourge of Kentucky and parts of Tennessee from 1885 into the early 1890s, and a similar creature would briefly resurface in Georgia in 1896. The Dog Eater's description often varied but was usually described as a quadrupedal mammal. Its size would also differ, as is to be expected, and witnesses could never seem to make up their minds whether it was a panther, a huge dog, or even a bear.

THAT MOST WONDERFUL ANIMAL.

Depiction of the Dog Eater from the
October 28, 1893 *Evening Times.*

It had the odd habit of attacking and eating other dogs as opposed to livestock most times, hence the name. In one eerie instance, it didn't eat the carcass but drained it of blood like a vampire. Though there were several cases where a large predatory animal was killed and passed off as the "Dog Eater," chances are that the real cryptid was actually multiple animals, nor were any of the slain carcasses likely that of the strange, almost supernatural "Dog Eater."

As it stands, the Dog Eater is not a terribly well-remembered cryptid, which may be why no one ever connected it to a chilling series of animal deaths in Bladenboro, North Carolina, in the mid-

1950s. The story of what is today called the Bladenboro Beast is a beat-for-beat retelling of the notorious Dog Eater in many ways. Like the Dog Eater, descriptions of the Bladenboro Beast varied between that of either a huge wolf or panther. The beast went after dogs and often drained them of blood, leading the creature to be called a "vampire" in the press. Perhaps the biggest difference between the Dog Eater and the Bladenboro Beast is that the latter was highly publicized and is today better remembered in cryptid circles.

Bladen County School after construction was finished in Bladenboro c.1939 under the WPA.

The killings got off to an inauspicious beginning on December 29, 1953, when a "sleek, black, [animal] about 5 feet long" killed a dog in Clarkton, North Carolina, eight miles from Bladenboro. By the 31st, what would later be dubbed the Bladenboro Beast made it to Bladenboro where it killed two dogs. The owner of the dogs, Johnny Vause, told the papers that they were "torn into ribbons and crushed" in an article printed the next day. Though the creature would be given many names, the article ironically picked the one that would stick right off the bat as it was titled "The Beast Of Bladenboro - They All Know It'll Come Back." The article went on to quote Vause:

My dogs put up a good fight. There was blood all over the porch, big puddles of it. And there was a pool of saliva on the porch. It killed one dog at 10:30 and left it lying there. My dad wrapped the dog up in a blanket. That thing came back and got that dog and nobody's seen the dog since. At 1:30 in the morning, it came back and killed the other dog and took it off. We found it three days later in a hedgerow. The top of one of the dog's heads was torn off and its body was crushed and wet, like it had been in that thing's mouth. The other dog's lower jaw was torn off.

Over the first few nights of January, the animal struck again and again, always killing dogs. One witness, D.G. Pait, said he watched from a service station as the beast attacked a dog and drug it into the woods. Pait didn't get a good look at the creature, but others described it as being like "a bear or a panther" about "three feet long, twenty inches high, with a long tail and a cat's face."

Others only heard the terrifying screams of the animal emanating from the swampland, which they said sounded like "a woman with a knife stuck in her back." Things got even weirder after an autopsy performed on one of the dogs found that "there wasn't more than two or three drops of blood in him..." in an article headlined "Vampire Tendencies Found In Bladenboro's 'Monsters'".

'Vampire' Charges Woman

BLADENBORO, Jan. 5—A large marauding cat that has killed and sucked the blood of at least seven dogs charged a woman here tonight, but turned and fled back into a swamp when she screamed and her husband rushed onto the scene.

Police Chief Roy Forbes said the animal charged into the yard of Mrs. C. E. Kinlaw when she went out onto her front porch to investigate whimpering dogs in the street.

After the incident occurred, the armed posse that went out tonight to track down and kill the "vampire" swelled to some 500 people and scores of dogs.

Mrs. Kinlaw, who lives in the mill village near Bladenboro Mills on Highway 211 one mile west of

here, said she heard the dogs whimpering early tonight and went to investigate.

Near the dogs, she said, was what looked like "a big mountain lion." It raced from three doors down the dirt street in front of her house to a few feet from her porch, then turned back when she screamed and her husband rushed out of the house, she said. A neighbor also came to her aid.

Chief Forcs said tracks in the dirt road in front of the Kinlaw home were "bigger than a silver dollar."

A search party from Wilmington which tracked the animal last night as it moved in a three-mile circle along the edges of swampy areas found tracks which revealed claws

See 'VAMPIRE.' Page Six.

By January 5, 1954, a pet rabbit had fallen victim to the beast and it was "cleanly decapitated and still warm" when found. That same night, the monster also charged a woman. This incident, more than anything, seemed to be what made the beast finally take off in the press. After the 5th, articles on the Bladenboro Beast appeared almost daily in papers across the country.

On January 5, 1954, the *Raleigh News and Observer* published a story entitled "'Vampire' Charges Woman." It described the so-called vampire as a "large marauding cat" that had recently "killed and sucked the blood of at least seven dogs." Mrs. C. E. Kinlaw witnessed the animal in action from her front porch, located in what was called the Mills Section near Bladenboro. Mrs. Kinlaw heard her dogs outside whimpering, and when she stepped out to investigate, she saw the strange animal which began to charge at her.

The paper reported that,

Near the dogs, she said, was what looked like "a big mountain lion." It raced from three doors down the dirt street in front of her house to a few feet from her porch, then turned back when she screamed and her husband rushed out of the house, she said. A neighbor also came to her aid.

By the time Police Chief Roy Fores had arrived, the animal had disappeared into a nearby swamp. The paper reported, "After the incident occurred, the armed posse that went out tonight to track down and kill the 'vampire' swelled to some 500 people and scores of dogs."

The search party had come from Wilmington with a pack of hunting dogs and was led by Lloyd Clemons, who had seen the monster previously in the same area. Clemons described it as being "dark in color" and "around three feet long, and low to the ground, probably 18-21 inches high." The tail, he said, was about 34 inches long.

Though they never found the creature itself, Clemons and his hunting party discovered prints that night "which revealed claws" as they tracked the animal "as it moved in a three-mile circle along the edges of swampy areas." Chief Fores also found tracks in the dirt road in front of the Kinlaw house that he said were "bigger than a silver dollar."

Armed Hunting Party To Seek Bladenboro's 'Vampire Beast'

BLADENBORO, N. C. (⅌) — A "vampire beast" that sucks blood from its victims had Bladenboro citizens up in arms today.

Armed posses roamed the town after the discovery of three mutilated dog bodies recently. Police Chief Roy Fores said the body of the latest victim was opened yesterday and it contained only a few drops of blood.

He said the three dogs all had their bottom lips broken open and their jawbones smashed back. He said the ear of one dog was chewed off and the tongues of the others chewed out.

Fores said the vampire probably is a mad wolf.

beast,' indicated this morning that the animal could be a huge wildcat or mountain lion.

Tracks leading away from the latest dog killing obviously were not those of a dog. Observers say they were spoors evidently left by a huge mountain lion, probably weighing between 80-100 pounds.

The tracks, deeply imprinted even in a hard grain field, led away from the latest dog killing in the community. Last night a puppy owned by Johnny Vause was killed, the seventh dog in that section to be a victim of the mysterious killer. The puppy last night, although not killed vampire fashion, had it's nose chewed off.

The *Robesonian* printed its own article on the animal, titled "Armed Hunting Party To Seek Bladenboro's 'Vampire Beast'" that same day. It, too, played up the vampire angle, beginning with the teaser that a "'vampire beast' that sucks blood from its victims had Bladenboro citizens up in arms today."

The article reported more so on the Bladenboro Beast's exploits before its run-in with Mrs. Kinlaw. Notably, it detailed the strange circumstances of the slayings of three of the dead dogs found recently. Chief Fores stated that all the dogs "had their bottom lips broken open and their jawbones smashed back" and that "the ear of one dog was chewed off and the tongues of the others chewed out." However, the most startling detail was that during an autopsy, one of the dogs had been "opened yesterday and it contained only a few drops of blood." (It should be noted that a later article revealed that the other three dogs were also later confirmed to be drained of blood.) The brief article ended with Fores speculating that the "vampire" was probably just a "mad wolf."

The same section continued with an article from reporter John Gause, who speculated that rather than a wolf, the beast seemed to be a mountain lion. Gause recorded that "Tracks leading away from the latest dog killing obviously were not those of a dog. Observers say they were spores evidently left by a huge mountain lion, probably weighing between 80-100 pounds." The tracks were "deeply imprinted even in a hard grain field, led away from the latest dog killing in the community."

After the incident with Mrs. Kinlaw, Fore issued a statement that he was "definitely worried" because an "animal of that size could very easily attack a child . . . even a grown man."

The article continued that another "armed hunting party with dogs was to be formed again today" on January the 5th. It also reported a few more sightings of the mysterious creature, which were again described as being cat-like. "Two carpenters [saw] the animal late yesterday afternoon but couldn't offer any description," the article concluded.

By this point the town had been worked into a frenzy. At the time, Chief Fores was quoted as saying that "the town was quieter now than he has ever known it." Fores added, "People stay off the streets and lock their doors now." In recent years, North Carolina Ghosts contacted a resident, Ev Butler, who was a young man at the time. He told them that "Night time was the feared time around these parts. As the sun set, the entire community on the west side of town went indoors and didn't come out unless necessary."[8]

As the hunt for the beast intensified, the *Robesonian* of the 6th reported that "Worried parents kept a close eye on their children here today as a strange 'vampire' beast continued to roam the countryside." The article went on to say that the "vampire apparently is some species of the cat family that is a blood sucker." The article also speculated that since two pairs of tracks were found on the night that the beast charged Mrs. Kinlaw that perhaps there were two creatures on the loose, presumably a mated pair. The new article also updated the populace on the second hunt, which took place on the night of the 5th. It stated that it comprised of "nearly 500 men and dogs" and as they "searched, last night, the animal struck, dragging a dog into the swamps within 100 feet of the searchers."

---

8 https://northcarolinaghosts.com/piedmont/beast-bladenboro/

By the morning of the 6th, Chief Fores stated that he and his posse of "some 20 armed men" would work "from now on if necessary" to "put a stop to the cat menace". The papers reported that the plan was to "surround a bay area about a mile from town, where the cat-like 'vampire beast' last struck" and set up traps there. Since the beast liked dogs, that's exactly what it would be baited with: a live canine. (Something similar to the hunt for the Dog Eater was implemented wherein a live dog was used as bait to try and lure the creature into the hunters' sights, by the way.)

Mrs. Kinlaw was interviewed again by the press at this time, and she finally gave her own distinct description of the beast. Rather than saying it looked like a cat, from what she could tell, "it looked like a dog from the rear" and it "appeared to be gray" in color. The paper added that "Understandably excited, she didn't observe the animal close enough to offer definite description."

An article in the *Panama City News* of the 7th was mostly repetitious of everything previously reported aside from a new detail in the concluding paragraph:

Fores said one man from the Wilmington area said he had spied a black panther in the forest near Wilmington about a year ago and that forest- fires may have driven the beast toward this area. Others believed it was a wolf or large wild dog.

CALTON FLOWERS of 501 Carthage road doesn't want to asso-
ciate the above pictured bobcat with anything that might be
frightening Bladenboro folks, but he thinks it's a pretty good kill
for his new gun. Mr. Flowers was duck hunting in Big Swamp,
just below Lennon's bridge Saturday morning at daybreak when
he heard the cat scream. At first thinking it was a woman's
scream, he beached his boat and went ashore. Soon the big 25-
pound cat came stalking slowly by and Mr. Flowers shot him down
with No. 6 shot from about 35 yards. It was the first kill for his
new shotgun.

On the 8th came a slew of articles from the *Robesonian* along with the unfortunately grainy image shown above. The collection of articles was dubbed "Kitty Corner" that day. It presented a particularly interesting selection of stories as they offered up every tidbit of information available on the creature and proposed a bevy of monikers for it including the Bladenboro Banshee, Bladenboro Boogie, the Bladenboro Breeder Beast, and so on. The articles offered up some new information on the creature, specifically more details as to the noises that it made, described as sounding "like a woman in pain," "barking like a coyote," and "crying like a baby."[9]

One of the articles gave the update that:

The catlike beast, possibly a maddened, panther accompanied by a mate, has killed at least six dogs in the Cotton Mill Hill area. Another dead-dog was found yesterday but Police Chief Roy Fores said it had not been established that the dog fell victim to the maddened beast.

Still another dog was spirited into the swamps as helpless residents listened to its death screams. Hundreds of gun-bristling volunteer hunters swarmed into the tiny mill town of about 800 population, making it difficult for professional hunters and their dogs to trap the killer. Police feared the volunteer help would shoot each other.

As events spiraled towards a much-needed conclusion, sporadic reports came in of the monster having been captured or killed only for those claims to turn out to be false. Likewise, dog

---

[9] This could be purely coincidental, but skinwalkers are often said to utter cries similar to a distressed person or a crying child.

deaths completely unrelated to the beast were also attributed to it. The only thing of real substance reported was that large four-toed tracks had been found in the front yard of E. B. Martin along Oakridge Ave. "The most distinct footprint measured about four inches in length and was about three inches wide, it clearly showed the outline of four toes," the paper reported. Around this time, as reports of the monster gained more and more publicity, others came from out of the woodwork with their own sightings. "Rogers Mathews has proof that the Bladenboro Boogie visited Robeson county first," one paper reported, then continued on that:

Several days before the varmint showed in Bladenboro, the beast slew three kittens at the Mathews home, badly mutilating their heads and necks. And a few days later a small lamb was also slain at the Mathews home, also being stacked in the face. It is believed to have proceeded from there to Bladen county. The Mathews have only 21 kittens left.

A strange animal was then seen by Roy Shipman of Lumberton, also in Robeson County. He described the animal as "having much bushy hair about the head and neck, but seemed to be clean shaven from the neck back, and had a long tail." Shipman saw it "crossing a field from Red Springs road" towards the local hospital as it carried a dog in its jaws. However, a report that came out a day later implied that the sighting was merely a hoax. As always, the waters were becoming muddied. Perhaps rather forebodingly, one article concluded with this paragraph:

> One famous animal trainer, who also prefers to remain anonymous, said he would capture the beast, train it to do right, patent his accomplishment, and sell it to Robeson and Bladen towns for Chamber of Commerce use.

Davis   'The Beast'   Fussell
... end of the vampire?

Luther Davis and Mayor Woodrow Fussell poses with the bobcat.

A bit like the scene in *Jaws* when every local with a boat sets sail to kill the deadly shark, Chief Fores and the mayor of Bladenboro, Bob Fussell, eventually decided that things were getting out of hand. As such, they called an end to the hunt and, also like in *Jaws*, this resulted in a false culprit being apprehended. While in *Jaws* it was a Tiger Shark, in Bladenboro a bobcat was killed on the 13th. That day, Luther Davis, a local farmer, had found the animal struggling in a steel trap in a swamp near the city and shot it in the head. Mayor Fussel then swiftly told the press that it was the Bladenboro Beast. To emphasize the point further, the carcass was swiftly strung up on the town flagpole which proclaimed, "This is the Beast of Bladenboro."

Luther Davis poses with the bobcat he killed.

But you know that it wasn't. The *Lumberton Robesonian* reported a story entitled "New 'Vampire' Rumors Fail To Excite Bladenboro

Chiefon" on January 15, 1954, on the front page. Despite reports of what some called "a giant 90-pound leopard cat" being killed, Chief Fores clarified that "the animal was actually a small bobcat run over near the Bladenboro school by Bunn Soles of Tabor City." The article continued that "Bladenboro hunters, although not active and organized, still are trying to trap the beast..." Fores was also not overly concerned with reports that the beast had struck yet again. Supposedly, three more dogs had been killed when, in fact, they were simply missing.[10]

Even though the little bobcat killed by Luther Davis most likely was not the Bladenboro Beast, after that the creature did seem to fade away. Some even think it was a bizarre publicity stunt

---

[10] Postulated within the same article was the idea that the Bladenboro Beast wasn't a feline, but a canine. "The theory that the mysterious Beast of Bladenboro might be a vicious, blood-hungry, escaped watchdog remains unproved," the article reported, and added, "However, the opinion that the mysterious beast is a huge panther or mountain lion also remains pure speculation."

The killer-dog theory had been advanced by a Lumberton veterinarian, Dr. N. G. Baird, who felt it was a "cross-bred watch dog" that had become "blood-hungry and killed some neighborhood chickens." As for Fores, he "still couldn't convince himself the beast is a dog." The dog in question was a German Shepherd and Hound mix named Big Boy belonging to a Native American youth who lived along the edge of Big Swamp (where the beast's cries were often heard). It was the opinion of the dog's former owner, A. R. Stanton, that it was the Bladenboro Beast as it had turned somewhat vicious whereas other animals were concerned.

aided along by the mayor, who not coincidentally operated the town theater. Suspiciously, he even stated that "a little publicity never hurts a town." Years later, he further claimed that the creature was "about 90% imagination, 10% truth." What really didn't help matters was the fact that Mayor Fussel just happened to book a movie called *The Big Cat* to be shown at his theater the week that media interest peaked!

And yet, that said, sightings continued. Newspaper columnist W. Horace Carter claimed to see the creature with his own eyes as reported in his column, Carter's Corner, in the May 5, 1954 edition of the *Tabor City Tribune*. He stated that while driving through Elizabethtown on the way to nearby Bladenboro he saw the animal himself. His account is as follows:

We came back through Elizabethtown and headed toward Bladenboro about 11:30 or a quarter to twelve. About two miles off of Elizabethtown a huge cat-like animal pounced out of the woods in the right some 100 feet in front of the car, made two huge leaps and completely crossed the highway directly in front of us.

The animal was no bobcat. It had a long tail that appeared to be about half the length of the car itself. It was about 20 to 24 inches in height, and I would guess from the rapid appearance that it weighed something like 50 pounds. It was a tan colored creature.

Jim Phillips and E.J. Britt, the Lumberton friends who were also in the car each got a good look at the animal. We make no claims that it was the long lost "Beast of Bladenboro" but we are sure of one thing, we haven't seen a creature like it before and we aren't hankering to come face to face with it without the benefit of an automobile's protection.

Nearly a year since the attacks began, the beast made headlines again, this time in Robeson. *The Robesonian*, who had reported on the Bladenboro killings with glee nearly a year ago, ran a story entitled "'Beast of Bladenboro' Type Killer Strikes in Robeson" on December 15, 1954. It reported how a "mysterious animal" had killed "five medium-sized pigs and three chickens, on K. M. Biggs tenant farm" near the Robeson Memorial hospital.

Marvin McLamb, who oversaw the farm, stated that he was awakened the night of the killings around midnight when his dogs began to bark. McLamb and his father then went outside to trail the disturbance with one of the dogs. The paper stated that as McLamb followed his dog, it stopped and became mysteriously frightened. The paper said, "When McLamb came up to the point the dog had trailed, the dog was whimpering. It then bolted for the house. McLamb said he too returned to the house."

The next morning, the pigs were found mutilated and strewn around a sty. Four of the pigs had crushed skulls and three of them had their legs torn from their bodies. "Strangely enough, no blood was evident, indicating the killer employed the same blood-sucking traits as the Bladenboro beast," the story reported. Tracks were also found which led to a small bay area, behind Meadowbrook Cemetery.

Of the large mysterious tracks the beast left in its wake, Mclamb said, "I don't think they are dog tracks." A neighbor, Worth Pittman, concurred with this statement, as the "spoor was four inches from heel to toe." The paper also clarified that the pigs were enclosed "in a regular board type sty with the boards nailed close enough together to prevent the passage of an animal indicated by the size of the track" and that the fence "was approximately four feet high."

Anticlimactically, a stray dog was killed and the County Dog Warden stated that it was "most probably" the killer reported in the news the night before. Never mind that the tracks found at the farm were never compared to the dead strays, nor was it explained how the dog could have reached the chickens, which were roosting up in a tree. A dog would not have scaled the tree, but a feline similar to the Bladenboro Beast would have.

VAMPIRE? Yes, says Dog Warden Carroll Freeman, right, who shot the dog about one-half mile from the place five pigs were mutilated Tuesday night. With the death of the mongrel, which weighed 65 pounds the 'beast' case was closed. At left is Charles Barnes, who accompanied Freeman in search of his own lost dog.
Robesonian Staff Photo by Gause

Even the local papers were skeptical of the dog story. An article entitled "'Beast of Bladenboro'

Scare Ends In Death Of Large Dog" noted that County Dog Warden Carol Freeman admitted that the slain dog's paws "were not compared to 4-inch spoors found around the farm, but Freeman said he thought they were large enough to be the same."

The article also noted the bit about the chickens, reporting that McLamb made clear that the dead chickens were taken from a roost in a tree. "The Dog Warden didn't attempt to explain how a dog could be responsible," the paper stated. As to blood drinking, "since no blood was observed around the small sty," Freeman stated that "a blood-thirsty dog would lap up warm blood."

The article also recorded that

> Warden Raymond Kinlaw predicts there will be further cases of such killings as long as some people feed raw meat to their dogs. "It definitely would cause a dog to become blood-thirsty," commented Kinlaw.

Though this is where most summarizations of the legend end, there is still an even stranger turn to the story. On December 17th was reported in *The Robesonian* that a strange creature was sighted at the Panthersford Elementary School by the students and the staff alike. The article reported that,

> An elementary school principal and one of his teachers said yesterday afternoon a mysterious animal which "looked like a cross between a

big monkey and a dog" was chased off the Panthersford school yard Wednesday by a group of students and a janitor armed with an axe.

The principal was H. E. Williams and the teacher was Christine McMillan. The animal was first spotted by a group of youngsters during a chapel program and, according to the teacher, "at least 25 of the kids ran outdoors to see what it was."

Panthersford is a Negro elementary school located between Lumberton and Red Springs on highway 211. The school is approximately 10 miles from the site of the recent mutilation of five young hogs on a farm near Lumberton by what is thought to have been a big dog.

ATTRACTED BY YELL

The teacher said she was first attracted to the animal's presence in the school yard by student Beula May Sanders' yell: "Look, a monkey!" There was an immediate scramble by the students to get a closer look.

The time was approximately 3 o'clock in the afternoon, according to Miss McMillan. When the school's janitor, Clifton Williams, saw the commotion and spied the animal, he picked up an axe.

Principal Williams said he didn't see the action take place, but from what he could learn from spectators, it didn't appear the animal showed any fear of the janitor.

"It would run when they ran," he explained, "but when they (the children and janitor) stopped running, it stopped, also." He said he understood the janitor got close enough to the strange beast to swing the axe but the animal dodged the blow and ran off.

Miss McMillan said she saw the animal plainly at a distance of about 50 feet. "It looked just like a big monkey and a dog, I don't know which. It didn't run, it loped."

She said the animal appeared to be colored "a dark, reddish brown." It was about "three feet" high and had an "extremely long tail."

Supt. Williams said he went out to examine the animal's tracks and found them unlike any he had ever seen. "But they definitely were not dog tracks," he exclaimed. He added, "and I certainly know what a dog track looks like."

DESCRIPTION DIFFERS

The children, said Williams, differed on a concrete description of the animal but agreed it wasn't a dog. Some said it was a monkey.

A beast scare in Robeson began Tuesday with the strange death of five medium sized hogs which were ripped and torn apart in a pigpen on a K. M. Biggs farm near Robeson Memorial hospital.

A 65-pound mongrel dog was killed in the vicinity the following day by Dog Warden Carroll Freeman and the case was closed.

The report of the monkey-like animal is reminiscent of the recent 'Beast of

Bladenboro' scare which produced many varied and weird reports of strange beasts roaming the country-side seeking prey.

The infamous 'Bladenboro Beast' was never positively identified but it was presumed to be either a cat-like swamp animal or a blood-thirsty dog.

Whatever the animal, or animals, it apparently doesn't like to fool around with humans. It operates under the cover of darkness and operates silently.

And with that, for the most part, the Bladenboro Beast was gone. True, a smattering of killings here and there would be blamed on the mystery beast, but never to the extent that they were between 1953 and 1954. And, if the creature wasn't the admittedly rather small bobcat killed around the 13th of January in 1954, what was it?

Due to its ever-changing appearance, some have wondered if the Bladenboro Beast may have been a shapeshifter of some kind. Balk if you want, but at the exact same time in rural Mexico, death certificates by the dozens were being turned in for infants citing the cause of death as "sucked by the witch." Babies in Tlaxcala were often found dead, they said, drained of blood by a shapeshifting witch. Said witch could transform into a turkey and also a cat-like creature if it wished when it came to prey upon the young children. Though it may sound like a bit of folklore, the Mexican government took it seriously enough to launch an investigation into the matter. Perhaps it's just coincidental, but it's interesting that it happened around the same time as the Bladenboro incident.

Real or not, the Bladenboro Beast has become the town mascot and there is even an annual "Beast Fest" held every year around Halloween.

In addition to the vampiric witch of Tlaxcala, one could also compare the Bladenboro Beast to a Navajo Skinwalker. Quasi-similar to the werewolf, a skinwalker is a witch that wears an animal pelt to transform into an animal. Sometimes these transformed creatures can appear quasi-humanoid. Remember the last account, where witnesses described the head as monkey-like? Going with our shapeshifter theory, what if what they were likening to a monkey was actually a human's face in mid-transition? Furthermore, the Bladenboro Beast's cry sounds a bit similar to that of a skinwalker's. According to skinwalker lore, the Navajo witches will sometimes utter a helpless cry like that of a baby crying or a woman in distress.

Of course, the more likely explanation is that the beast was simply an unidentified predator that was never captured and moved on to other parts. Or, for the most dissatisfying answer of all, maybe it was just a hoax perpetrated by the town? As with most of the mysteries covered in this book, we will likely never know.

5

ATTACK OF THE
DINOSAUR MEN
A Tale of a Tribe with Tails

EVERY SO OFTEN in folklore comes tales of men with tails. Historically speaking, the long queues worn by the Doriri of British New Guinea begat rumors that there was a race of "tailed men" living there. That said, very, very rarely can a human being be born with a "tail," which is basically a form of spinal dysraphism. According to medical literature, only 40 cases of true human tails have ever been recorded, and the longest measured only about seven inches. However, the tails on the race of men about to be described were much longer than that and much more reptilian. And, in all likelihood, they probably weren't real.

The story of Alaska's "tailed men" was told by a man named Reverend Arthur R. Wright, who served as a missionary in Alaska in the early 1900s. According to Ed Ferrell's book *Strange Stories of Alaska and the Yukon*, Wright was "half Athabaskan, the son of a white man and an Indian mother."[11] Ferrell went on to say that even though Wright collected many myths from the native peoples, they spoke of the story of the tail men as being something real.

Man fishing in Copper River.
(Date unknown, taken prior to 1930 by John Nathan Cobb)

The story was published in the *Cordova Daily News* of February 7, 1924:

The Tail Men

On a recent trip over to the Copper River the Indians drew my attention to numerous holes

---

[11] Ferrell, *Strange Stories*, p.43.

in an embankment we passed. On inquiring of them I was told that those were the holes of "men with tails." With some questioning, this is the tale I heard.

In the Selina River country were rolling hills on which numerous caribou roamed. The Indians who subsisted on meat were lured to this district by the abundance of game. And years ago at the mouth of the Selina River they built a large Indian village.

One day a dog brought into the camp the tail of a fish. No one had caught any fish, and it puzzled the Indians as to how the animal got the fish. Finally it was decided to search the district to determine if there were any other tribes in the area.

A group went out to search for the unknown people. When several of the searchers did not return, the tribe knew something was wrong.

What had happened to these men?

Finally one of their most skillful trackers was sent in search of the missing scouts.

He made his way cautiously through the country. At length he came upon a hidden trail through the woods. Across the path at intervals was stretched a rope made of grass. This he examined very carefully.

"A trap... An alarm," he thought.

He continued to follow the trail, which led to a group of caves he could see in the distance.

Very cautiously he strained eye and ear for sight or sound of anything unusual. Finally from out of the numerous caves came men with tails. They had all the appearance of normal men except for a tail, which dragged behind them. He was much surprised to see them use these tails as their chief means of locomotion. They curled their tails forward between their legs and recoiled in such a manner as to push themselves forward.

As the scout watched them, keeping up wind to avoid being detected by scent, they kicked what looked to him like a ball. On observing it more closely, the Indian recognized to his horror the head of one of his companions.

He watched them rush to and fro, capering about with much shouting and hideous glee, evidently having a game of ball with the head.

He quickly noted their number, also the number of caves, and returned back to his camp.

After he made his report, a group of men and boys gathered, and an attack was planned on the village of Tail Men. They decided to seal off the caves with fire and smoke, thus killing the people inside.

It was raining when they reached the caves and the Tail Men were all inside. Each group was detailed to a cave. With burning brands and brush, the Indians rushed the caves and plugged the openings.

As the attackers stood guard, through the fire came flights of arrows. Soon this stopped. After all signs of life from the Tail Men had ceased, the Indians returned homeward.

The Tail Men were no more a menace to the Indians. Today all that remains of them are this legend, their caves, and numerous arrowheads.

Thus ended the story, and someday I hope to return and try to find out more about these Tail Men.

Ferrell notes in his book that he is unaware if Reverend Wright ever sought out the caves for himself. As for what the tribe of people could have been if they existed at all, there really aren't any reports of similar humanoids apart from Lizard Men and Reptilian aliens. However, the humanoids in this chapter were described as looking like normal humans apart from their tails. Due to its one-off nature and more fantastic attributes, this one seems more likely to be a hoax or a simple folktale.

Sources:

Ferrell, Ed. *Strange Stories of Alaska and the Yukon*. Epicenter Press, 1996.

Man Reports 'Big Bird' Attack

RAYMONDVILLE, Tex (AP) — A Raymondville man told officers he was attacked by a "big bird" as he stood in the back yard of his home late Wednesday, police said Thursday.

Earlier, several persons in the Lower Rio Grande Valley, including two police officers, reported sighting a large birdlike creature with a wing spread of 10-15 feet, large eyes and a bat-like face.

A spokesman for the Willacy County Sheriff's office said Armando Grimaldo, about 26, told them a big black bird with big eyes and a monkey-like face attacked him and tore his jacket and shirt. The man was taken to a local hospital for treatment and was released after hospital attendants could not find any trace of physical injury.

Grimaldo was at home in bed Thursday, reportedly in shock, and would not discuss the incident with newsmen.

"His wife called us and told us he had been beaten up by a big bird," a city police spokesman said. The officer who went to see Grimaldo said "he was pretty scared and was shaking," a spokesman said.

Neighbors told reporters that Grimaldo told them he was standing in his back yard when he "felt some wind and looked up and this big bird attacked him." The neighbors said they didn't see anything when they went outside after hearing Grimaldo scream.

TEXAS PTEROSAUR FLAP
Big Bird in the Big Bend Country

IN THE EARLY MONTHS of 1976, when most states were gearing up for America's Bicentennial celebration, Texas was amidst a true flap of an avian cryptid, dubbed the "Big Bird" in the press. The creature was glimpsed many times throughout the winter, though the most attention was given to a sighting that occurred on February 24th for good reason. In the case of that encounter, the big bird was clearly a pterosaur as opposed to simply a large bird as the monster's moniker in the press implied.

Three schoolteachers were driving down an isolated road southwest of San Antonio when a huge shadow passed over them. In their opinion, the creature casting the shadow resembled the prehistoric pterodactyl. However, to many others, namely the "experts," the bird was simply an overgrown pelican.

Whatever it was, the Big Bird was seen by many residents in Southeastern Texas near the border. For some, the "Big Bird" took on a supernatural connotation, a sign of bad luck or oncoming misfortune. Texas nature columnist Hazel Green even stated that there was a "general feeling it is not of this World." Others likened it to UFO sightings, but for cryptozoologists, specifically those interested in remnant dinosaurs, the bird offered what could be one of the first pterosaur sightings in the U.S. since the infamous Tombstone Thunderbird case of 1890.

Generally speaking, the overlapping consensus was that it was five to six feet tall with a 10-15-foot wingspan, a long beak, and a color that varied between black, white, and grey. Notably, most sightings occurred at night. Though not applicable to every sighting, some witnesses gave the creature long legs, a long neck, a bat-like face, and large, red shiny eyes about the size of a silver dollar. The long beak alternated in size, with some having it as small as six inches, while others said it was four feet long.

Though the publicity wave for the Big Bird began in January of 1976, there had actually been sightings before that. In September of 1975, an unidentified man called in to a radio station to describe a sighting he had of several large birds while fishing near a sand bar out from the mouth of the San Bernard River. He claimed to have seen eight tall figures that he at first mistook for fisherman wading into the river. However, as he got closer to them, within about 200 yards, he saw that they were, in fact, "huge birds like he never saw before."[12] The man didn't report the creatures for fear that people would think him crazy and only came forward after others did the same with their "Big Bird" stories. The man also made it clear they were not pelicans, as he had observed plenty of them in his lifetime.

Another caller on what was presumably the same program reported a sighting on December 13, 1975, near Los Fresnos. While no photographic evidence was ever produced of the big bird, photos were said to have been taken of its tracks. Hazel Green reported in her "Nature Notes" column that she had heard:

> Two men from the TV station offering the $1,000 reward were on the line being interviewed. They said they had pictures of about 80 yards of huge bird tracks in a freshly plowed field near Harlingen. This was not far from where the 3-toed prints 9" wide were found. Unfortunately I heard only a part of this program.[13]

Sometime before the New Year, two police deputies in Harlingen, midway between Raymondville and Brownsville, sighted a huge

---

[12] Green, "Big Bird", *Wimberley Mill* (February 1, 1976).
[13] Ibid.

bird with a 10-foot wingspan glide over their patrol cars in the early morning hours. Initially, their sighting was brushed off as an unusually large pelican. On New Year's Day, two teenage girls, Tracy Lawson and Jackie Davies, spied a frightening, five-foot-tall "bird" leering at them in their yard as they played. The next day, their parents found large, three-toed tracks which were featured on a local news segment. (This was likely the same segment regarding the tracks mentioned a few paragraphs back.)

The broadcast was said to have aired on January 2nd, and coincidentally, perhaps foreshadowing things to come, on January 3rd a Valley TV station broadcasted *The Flying Serpent*. The 1946 horror film was based upon the legend of Quetzalcoatl, the flying serpent god of the Aztecs, and set in New Mexico.

The titular character in *The Flying Serpent* (1946).

The same day as the TV broadcast, two policemen spotted a large bird with 15-foot wing span gliding over San Benito. Arturo Padilla and Homero Galvan were traveling in separate squad cars when both saw the creature. "It more or less looked like a stork or pelican type of bird," Padilla said in the *McAllen Monitor* of January 12, 1976. "The wingspan I guess was about like a pretty good-sized car, about 15 feet or so. The color was white. I've done a lot of hunting but I've never seen anything like it." Their report, in turn, reminded San Benito police chief Ted Cortez that six weeks before, a terrified man had rushed into the station to report his own sighting of the giant bird.

After the broadcast, coupled with the San Benito sighting, the local press began to be flooded by questions and reports alike regarding the monster. "One TV man said he had been on duty from 4 a.m. to 9 p.m. to try and take care of all the calls," Hazel Green reported in her "Nature Notes" column.

Then, on January 7th, the most terrifying encounter yet took place. That night in Brownsville, Alverco Guajardo felt something slam into his trailer. Guajardo went outside to investigate and saw a monstrous bird, which he described to the press as "A bird, but not a bird like something from another planet!"

As Guajardo looked around outside, he made his way to his station wagon to make use of its headlights. When he switched them on, he beheld a terrifying apparition. The creature was black and stood about four feet tall wrapped in immense, bat-like wings. The eyes glowed red, and the bird-like entity possessed a beak that he estimated to be between two to four feet long. The creature let loose a piercing shriek and then backed out of the headlights and into the darkness. As for Guajardo, he sought shelter in a neighbor's home. Reportedly, when he told the press about the encounter the next day, he was still trembling.

An even more terrifying encounter followed on January 14th when the monstrous bird attacked a Raymondville resident, Armando Grimaldo, late that night. And, though Grimaldo's encounter was probably the most famous of the bunch, his wasn't the only one that took place on the 14th. Two young men fishing on the river saw the bird around sunset of the same day as recounted in an article entitled "'Big Bird' scares pair from river" in the *El Paso Herald Post* of January 15, 1976.

Big Bird

If this composite drawing of the "Big Bird" is anything like the real thing, it's no wonder that some of the people who have reported seeing it have been scared out of their wits. Many residents of Texas' Lower Rio Grande Valley have reported seeing the creature, claiming that it has a wingspan of about 15 feet. This composite was drawn by KRGV-TV staff artist Marianne Hartness from several descriptions of the "Big Bird." (UPI)

Illustration of the Big Bird appearing in the *El Paso Herald Post* (January 15, 1976).

The two witnesses were identified as 19-year-old Auturo Rodriguez and his nine-year-old nephew Ricardo. While fishing, just off the road and away from the hustle and bustle of the city, they were watching the sun set over the river when they heard an unfamiliar noise.

"It was like the rustling of leaves," Arturo told the press. Then the duo spotted a "giant grey bird" with a wingspan of 15 to 20 feet and a five-foot-long body gliding about 50 feet over the river.

After this, the two "ran like the Devil was after us. We didn't even say anything to each other until we reached the front door of the house."

Two hours later, 24-year-old Roberto Gonzalez was driving to Laredo along U.S. 83, which runs parallel the river. Near the oilfields he saw the creature sixty feet in the air "silhouetted against the clouds."

The same article went on to recount past sightings of the "Big Bird," including one as far back as June of 1975 in the El Paso area. Fifteen-year-old Gary Martinez was in the backyard of his parent's house when he heard the leaves begin to rustle. He turned around and spotted a huge white bird with a wingspan of fifteen feet coming from the west right towards him. Gary was so frightened of the creature that he hit the ground as it flew over. His mother was quoted in the article as stating that "He could feel the moving air from the wings as it flew over him, and he saw the dirt on the ground stir from the force of the moving air. He turned his head to look up and saw the huge wings beating slowly as the bird took on altitude and flew toward Ft. Bliss."

Gary ran inside after that to tell his parents of what he had just seen. Until the sightings of 1976, his parents didn't fully believe his accounts of just how big the bird was. (The paper also noted that Gary never got a good glimpse of the bird's head, just the underside of the body as it flew overhead.)

Dating back even further, the paper reported, was a sighting from five years ago by a man named Jesus Martinez of Donna, Texas. "It was about 16

96

feet wide because it covered the width of the road, I know it's no buzzard because I don't think a buzzard flies at night and it's much bigger than a buzzard," he told the press in 1976 because back in 1971 he was afraid of being laughed at.

However, those sightings paled in comparison to that of 26-year-old Armando Grimaldo of Raymondville on the night of January 14th. He had gone outside his mother-in-law's home to go smoke a cigarette in the backyard when he suddenly heard a flapping of great wings along with a sort of whistle. Before he knew it, he was accosted by a strange flying creature. Interestingly, it wasn't a perfect match for the one seen outside of Alverco Guajardo's trailer the week before outside of being roughly the same size of ten to fifteen feet. This entity, according to Grimaldo, had no beak. Instead, he likened the face to that of a monkey or a bat. Notably, though, the creature lacked feathers and had leathery skin.

In any case, one could forgive Grimaldo if his description of the creature didn't match that of other witnesses as he was in a state of great distress since the creature attempted to abduct him. Reportedly it swooped down and clawed at his back until he managed to get away. After, he was transported to the Willacy County Hospital in a state of shock. The *Abilene Reporter News* of January 16, 1976, featured the original account and stated that Grimaldo was "released after hospital attendants could not find any trace of physical injury."

As for statements from the police in the same article, they were quoted as saying, "His wife called us and told us he had been beaten up by a big bird" and that "he was pretty scared and was shaking."

The following day, Grimaldo was reportedly still in bed and in shock, refusing to discuss the incident with reporters, all of whom had to get their accounts from Grimaldo's wife and neighbors.

And yet, despite that terrifying account, over the next few days the press seemed to do everything they could to imply that the bird was nothing serious. *The San Antonio Light* ran a story mocking the incidents where they asked readers for their theories on what the big bird was. No one took it seriously, or perhaps the paper didn't publish the serious theories. Instead, it printed theories such as, "I am not sure, but I think the Big Bird is my first wife. It sure looks like her."

But still, sightings poured in. Two sisters claimed to spy Big Bird at a watering hole near Brownsville on the 18th and two ranch hands saw it the same day on a ranch near Poteet.[14] The two girls saw the creature near a pond and described it as being as tall as they were with a bat-like face. The ranch hands near Poteet said it was five feet tall and standing in the water of a stock tank. Interestingly, one of the witnesses, Jesse Garcia, told the press, "He started flying, but I never saw

---

[14] Other sources, specifically Jerome Clark's *Unexplained!*, say these two sightings happened on January 11, 1976.

him flap his wings. He made no noise at all." One could argue this sighting was almost supernatural and more in line with the likes of Mothman, but perhaps the creature simply leaped into the air and glided away without flapping its wings.

Lonely vigil

Ah, 'tis a lonely vigil that Hortense keeps as she awaits the return of her beloved Henry. The Abyssinian Ground Hornbills were once a cozy twosome in the Abilene Zoo until Henry flew to new heights and escaped. Could Abilene's favorite Henry Hornbill be the Big Bird that is reportedly terrorizing valley residents? (Staff Photo by Don Blakley)

The January 19, 1976 edition of the *Abilene Reporter News* wondered if Big Bird was simply Henry Hornbill, pictured above.

An article in the January 25, 1976, edition of the *Del Rio News Herald* had an article headlined "Big Bird for Real; At Least Del Rio's" by Ima Jo Fleetwood, which contained a further wealth of information. Her article revealed a sighting on Friday, January 23rd. Two teen boys, Victor Castillo and David Vasquez, were fishing along the San Felipe Creek "near Gillis and Losoya Streets" when "they saw a Big Bird flying by."

Their description of the creature was limited, simply describing it as "black and very big." They described its flight as being that of a gliding motion, sailing towards town in a westerly direction. The boys called the police, who told the paper that the boys "were very scared" when they arrived.

Though that description was rather vague, the article does have one of the best descriptions of the bird leaning towards the pterosaur theory. The creature was sighted by Jasper Kilroy in his backyard the following morning at about 5:45 A.M. The article said,

Kilroy resides across from the San Felipe Country Club's golf course off Bedeil and he said the bird was stalking around the backyard, making funny noises as if he were talking and saying "down with the pill." He said the bird had long legs, a long neck, no feathers and looked like a stork. He said it was greyish blue, appeared cold and seemed "about to starve to death." He said the bird, about 5 feet tall, flew off in a northeasterly direction, "toward San Angelo."

SAN BENITO, HOME OF THE BIG BIRD? — This interesting shelter was spotted by our bird editor recently on the West bank of the Resaca near the north frontage road along the expressway. He conjectured that it might be inhabited by the big bird, particularly since shortly after it was reported in other parts of Texas, the "bird nest" disappeared. (Staff Photo)

Big Bird clipping from the *San Benito News* of January 25, 1976.

The article then went on to relate that a resident, Barbara Petseh,

...who lives on Highway 90 West atop a hill that gives her a beautiful view for miles and miles, reported she had heard the Big Bird had been captured by someone who threw a net over it while it fought fiercely. The report, Barbara said, came from McAllen, where KK10 had offered $1,000 for its capture, but she couldn't verify it.

As more and more hunters voiced their desire to shoot "Big Bird," Ed Dutch, commission officer of the Texas Parks and Wildlife Department, issued the following warning:

> We have a number of species of birds that do exist in South Texas in the Valley area. Many of them have wingspans up to perhaps 10 feet or in excess of 10 feet, and some of them are on the rare endangered species list. The punishment for catching a protected bird could cost a hunter $5,000.

An article from the *Port Arthur News* of February 13, 1976, on page ten claimed that Big Bird was nothing but a Great Blue Heron. The paper said that "Some farmworkers spied Big Bird Wednesday roosting in a fruit orchard about two miles south of Alamo."

The paper continued that about 50 people had gathered within the hour to watch the bird. Among them was a television reporter who managed to film the bird "as it stood quietly watching the people mill around."

Dr. Don Farst, curator of the Gladys Porter Zoo in nearby Brownsville, claimed that the bird had been classified correctly as a Great Blue Heron, which was "not [an] uncommon visitor to the Rio Grande Valley."

However, the Big Bird would return in a very big way in eleven days. On February 24th, three school teachers driving down a lonely road outside of San Antonio saw it. One of the teachers, David

Rendon, is quoted in Jerome Clark's *Unexplained!* as saying:

> It just glided. It didn't fly. It was no higher than the telephone line. It had a huge breast. It had different legs, and it had huge wings, but the wings were very peculiar like. It had a bony structure, you know, like when you hold a bat by the wing tips, like it has bones at the top and in between.[15]

As soon as they could, the three witnesses looked through various textbooks in an effort to find the strange bird. They found their answer in one featuring dinosaurs, singling out a pterosaur as what best resembled the creature they saw.

Actually, what I recounted is the typical version of the tale. If one reads the original newspaper reports, one will find that the teachers actually saw two of the flying monsters. Furthermore, the teachers were also spilt up into two separate vehicles when the sighting occurred ten miles south of San Antonio. I found two distinct articles on the sighting, and although both overlap just a bit, each also has variations that serious armchair researchers like ourselves will no doubt find interesting. I will recount the more relevant bits starting with the *McAllen Monitor* of February 26.

That paper quoted Patricia Bryant as stating that the two creatures were as big as small airplanes and resembled prehistoric birds. Despite the

---

[15] Clark, *Unexplained!,* Kindle Edition.

sandhill crane identification of the previous Big Bird, Bryant was adamant that she had seen something more like a pterodactyl. The article quoted her as saying, "I have found a picture of a prehistoric bird that looks more like this thing than I've ever seen." Specifically, while scouring an encyclopedia, she found a picture of a pteranodon.

Ornithostoma ingens, 18 feet spread of wings, restored by Williston.

Image from *Outing* magazine (1908).

The paper went on to quote her as saying,

It was the biggest thing I've ever seen alive, particularly flying. My Lord, it (pteranodons)

lived like 160 million years ago. It's just unreal Where did it come from? I just don't know how it could have survived all those millions of years and still be flying around here. It's enough of a shock to see one then to discover there were two is really frightening.

It all happened so fast and it was such a shock you think you are seeing things. It was just enormous and frightening. I told my husband it was a big as a Piper Cub and he just laughed at me. I think the wing span was 15 or 20 feet if not more.

The paper went on to explain that the other two witnesses, David Hendon and Marsha Dahlberg, were in separate cars as one of the birds flew over them and "cast a shadow across the entire road." The teachers stopped their vehicles and then observed "another [bird] circling like a buzzard over a herd of cattle."

The article concluded with the statement that school officials had asked the teachers not to discuss their sightings on campus "for fear of alarming their pupils."

The other report was published in the *Rosenberg Herald Coaster* on March 2, 1976, and gave David Hendon's last name as that of Rendon this time. It also listed the witnesses' ages as 45 (Bryant), 22 (Rendon), and 25 (Dahlberg). It's important to note that the paper reported that in "separate interviews, they gave almost identical descriptions of the birds which Mrs. Bryant said resembled a [sic] pteradon". Interestingly, the paper also went on to describe past Big Bird sightings, noting its varying descriptions and that it alternately had the "face of a bat, monkey or human." (As for the teachers in this encounter, according to the article just quoted, they did not get a good look at the creature's head.)

One of the better quotes, again from Mrs. Bryant, stated, "This bird looks like it was half-reptile, half-bird. The wing had two joints in it like a chicken wing. I definitely saw it did have feathers. I could see the skeleton of this bird through the skin or feathers or whatever and it stood out black against the background of the grey feathers. It was the biggest thing I've ever seen alive, particularly flying. It all happened so fast and it was such a shock you think you are seeing things. It was enormous and frightening."

The article also quoted Rendon, who stated that, "We were afraid we were going to get ridiculed and criticized. I don't care what other people think. I saw it. I know it's true. It soared a couple of feet from the car. I've got a big car and it covered the whole thing. I swear to you that bird was going 30 to 40 miles an hour."

The sighting was enough to rile up Hazel C. Green's "Nature Notes" column again in the March 1, 1976, issue of the *Wimberly Mill*. In it, she surmised:

There have been hundreds of reported sighting and experiences with Big Bird from Harlingen, San Benito, McAllen, Raymondville, Rio Hondo, Los Fresnos,

Poteet, El Paso, Corpus Christi, San Antonio, and Laredo, that I know of. Two composite drawings have been made from two different sightings, both vastly different -- one that might be a Pelican, and another that fails to resemble any bird from this area or Texas.

There was no Big Bird news again that I know of until autumn, when *The Ennis Daily News* of September 23, 1976, reported that it had been sighted late Tuesday night near the Brazosport police station by Aaron Wilson. He described the bird as being as big as a car and he was about 100 yards away when he saw it. Another unidentified witness saw it that same night flying near the Brazos River Bridge. He estimated its wingspan at 28-30 feet.

That was the last major recorded sighting of the bird in 1976. However, Cryptopia did an excellent write-up on the Big Bird and apparently spoke to an additional witness named Alex Resendez, who saw the creature three times in the 1970s. His first two sightings were brief glimpses of the winged cryptid flying over Brownsville. Resendez's third sighting, in broad daylight near his McCook area home, is the interesting one, though—one that not coincidentally sheds some light on the monster's varying descriptions.

Resendez said he saw the big bird land near a cow pasture. He said that the eyes were a glassy black with very distinctive red markings around them. The body color, he said, was brown, and the creature stood about four feet tall, which was

consistent with other sightings. But it's the beak
that proved to be the most interesting. Remember
how some witnesses described a gigantic beak and
others no beak at all? Resendez told Cryptopia the
following:

> You have to look close because his beak is very
> transparent. If you see it real fast, you're going
> to think he ain't got no beak... I never seen a
> bird that big. He was brownish, like dirt... He
> does not have long legs and does not stand like
> other birds.[16]

Resendez said that the creature flew away when
an angry bull charged it. As it did so, Resendez
observed that the wings had blue and white stripes.

Although it's not said when Resendez had that
particular sighting, six years after the 1976 flap,
there was another major sighting in 1982. At 3:55
A.M. on September 14th, an ambulance
technician, James Thompson, was driving along
Highway 100 a little ways east of Los Fresnos,
Texas, midway between Harlingen and
Brownsville. About 150 feet ahead of him, he
witnessed a huge bird-like creature sail over the
highway at a low altitude. What struck him, in
addition to its great size, was its tail, which looked
like a fin of sorts.

The animal was a black or grayish color, and he
was sure that it lacked feathers. At the back of the
head, which he said seemed to have no neck, was

---

[16] https://www.cryptopia.us/site/2010/10/big-bird-texas-usa/

a bump that he likened to a Brahma bull. He also observed a pouch of some sort along the neck like a pelican. The wingspan he estimated at five to six feet, and the body itself at a length of eight. Like a pterodactyl, the wings appeared to have "indentations" on their tops and bottoms. He was so awestruck that he pulled over to watch the creature, which he expected to land in the manner of a model airplane due to the fact that it appeared to be gliding rather than flying. Instead of landing, it flapped its wings and took back to the sky. Like the teachers from six years before, he, too, found a picture of the animal in a book. It was a pterosaur.

When Thompson's sighting became public, once again the experts decided that he had glimpsed a large pelican or even an ultra-light flyer! According to Ken Gerhard's *Big Bird!*, a similar sighting was had around the same time in the Houston area by Richard Guzman and a friend only identified as Rudy. Together they observed a similar animal flying about fifty feet off the ground from a distance of 120 feet. Guzman provided Gerhard with a sketch of the creature, which had a distinct head crest similar to a pterodactyl, along with a long tail ending in a fin.

Douglas Lawson with Texas pterosaur fossil. (University of California at Berkeley, Bancroft Library; photographer Dennis Galloway)

Though pterosaurs have likely been glimpsed in the Texas skies since then, this is where we shall conclude our flap of the "Big Bird" of 1976. Whether pterosaurs soared the Texas skies of the late 1970s or not, they did inhabit the area in the prehistoric past. A large variety of pterosaur, *Quetzalcoatlus northropi*, was unearthed in the Big Bend region in 1971 by Douglas Lawson, a graduate student working with the Texas Memorial Museum's Dr. Wann Langston, Jr.

Today the skeleton hangs in the Great Hall of the Texas Natural Science Center's exhibit hall in the Texas Memorial Museum. If nowhere else in Texas, you're guaranteed to see a pterosaur there. Otherwise, when in the Big Bend region, keep watching the skies, just in case.

Sources:

Clark, Jerome. *Unexplained!: Strange Sightings, Incredible Occurrences & Puzzling Physical Phenomena.* Visible Ink Press; 3rd edition (September 1, 2012).

Morphy, Rob. "BIG BIRD: (TEXAS, USA)." Cryptopia (October 17, 2010).
https://www.cryptopia.us/site/2010/10/big-bird-texas-usa/

SIDE STORY

Horse-Headed Alligator

From page 16 of the *Logansport Pharos Tribune* of May 18, 1919, comes this odd lake monster report:

STRANGE REPTILE PLAYS HAVOC
WITH FISH NEAR MARION

MARION, Ind. May 18. -A reptile or animal of some strange species has taken up its abode in the waters of the Manzanita Fishing club pond in southern Fairmount and is causing havoc among fish put there by the club several years ago, according to persons living in the vicinity of the pond. Those who claim to have seen it say the creature has the head of a horse and the body of an alligator. Some of the people living near the pond even states they are disturbed by unearthly noises coining from the pond at times.

TYRANNOSAURS ALONG THE TRAIL
Depression Era Dinosaur Pet

PLESIOSAURS ARE COOL. So are pterodactyls as far as remnant dinosaurs go. But what everyone really wants to know is, has anyone ever seen a living tyrannosaurus rex? The answer to that question is...maybe. Though infrequent, T-rex sightings do occur, such as the Burrunjor in Australia. While the U.S. sports no truly credible adult T-Rex sightings, there are two notable instances of what could have been a baby T-rex recorded.

During his investigations into the Colorado River Dinos, Nick Sucik managed to unearth a witness who claimed he had found a baby T-rex in the wild. The man was an unnamed prospector in his mid-60s when Sucik interviewed him in the early 2000s. The man sighted the creature when he was a boy in May of 1951 while camping with his family along the Russian River in northern California.

"An Autumnal Sunset on the Russian River
Evening Glow" by William Keith (1878).

After taking a swim in the river, the boy waded over to get his clothes. On the shore, he saw what looked to be a dinosaur rather than a lizard. It stood erect with a human posture[17] at eight inches tall, with a much shorter three-inch tail. The reptile had a head just like the tyrannosaurs the boy had seen in picture books. He described it as being a very "ugly" head. It was rounded rather than pointed like a lizard or a snake's, and its teeth protruded from the mouth even when it was

---

[17] It's interesting that what the boy saw matched so perfectly in posture how dinosaurs were drawn in the 1950s. Whereas today dinosaurs are depicted hunched forward, the head in line with the tail, in the 1950s they were often depicted with upright human postures, and their tails dragged the ground.

closed. Further like a T-Rex, the arms were disproportionally short when compared to the legs. When he tried to grab it, the little dinosaur darted off, never to be seen again. The old prospector told Sucik that during his years of prospecting he "kept his ear to the ground" in hopes of hearing of other creature sightings like his but never did. Sucik summed up his entry on the creature, writing, "Still, he was haunted by one nagging question: what if the animal he had seen was merely a baby?"[18]

Was the creature seen by the old prospector just a baby version of the T-Rex?

[18] Sucik, "Dinosaur Sightings", *Cryptozoology and the Investigation of Lesser Known Mystery Animals*, p.162.

Typical Depression-Era Campsite.

Sucik discovered one other "baby T-rex" story when he was contacted by a man who told him a tale that his two aunts had told him. When the sisters were young girls during the Depression, they and their family traveled from state to state following the crop harvests. One night, as their mother was cooking at their camp, a reptile that the girls described as an "itty bitty T-rex" wandered into camp. Apparently the small creature came several times, and eventually the girls managed to capture it. The size of a small kitten, they kept it inside a birdcage and fed it scraps from their meals. The women said the teeth were sharp like a kitten's but that it was quite docile like "a tame squirrel." They said that it was peaceful but did not like to be held.[19] Like a T-rex, it had small arms with "hooks" and when it ran, it would lean forwards until it "flattened out" with its head in line with the tail. This detail in particular got Sucik's attention. This story was told to the nephew in the 1970s, a time when that posture was not widely accepted for dinosaurs. The story ended with the baby dinosaur outgrowing its cage. The girls' father instructed them to set it free once it was time to move onto the next crop harvest.

Along similar lines, there are rumors of a cryptid called the Mountain Boomer living in Big Bend National Park.[20] They are said to be five to seven feet tall and could be called pygmy tyrannosaurs at that height, considering most were 50 feet long. But, regardless of the smaller stature, they are described by witnesses as looking like tyrannosaurs. Additional details say that the creatures have large flaps of skin above and below the head. They get their name from the booming howl they emit. In the 1970s, John Keel even received a letter about one of these creatures running a car off of the road in the Big Bend area.

---

[19] On that note, the girls said the creature seemed to be warm blooded, which again lends credence to the theory that some dinosaurs were warm blooded. This even lines up with our friend, the Ceratosaurus of the Arctic Circle, covered in *Cowboys & Saurians: Ice Age.*

[20] These shouldn't be confused with the Mountain Boomer, a 14-inch Eastern Collared Lizard that can run on two legs. On that note, people have claimed to have seen giant versions of those, too.

Whether there be live dinosaurs in the Big Bend or not, dinosaur bones were found in the Big Bend dating back to 30 million years ago, when they should have been 65 million years old, meaning that yet another geologic anomaly was afoot.

Sources

Sucik, Nick. "Dinosaur Sightings." *Cryptozoology and the Investigation of Lesser Known Mystery Animals.* Coachwhip Publications, 2006.

SIDE STORY
A LOST WORLD IN OKLAHOMA?

Initially, I was quite excited by this story. However, as I began reading it, it simply seemed to be too good to be true. But, before telling you why it's a complete fabrication, take a look at the tale, which was printed in the *Cannelton Telephone* of May 16, 1918, on page three.

LOST WORLD FOUND, EXPLORER DECLARES

Expedition will scale heights in search of ancient animals and customs.

ARKANSAS CITY, Kan.— A lost world, inhabited by birds with leather wings and teeth, and thousands of other strange and weird creatures, has been found in the Osage Hills, in a wild and only partially explored section of Northwestern Oklahoma. The tale of the lost world was brought here by John Brune, a member of the Osage Indian tribe, who has a reputation as an explorer.

The story told by Brune is as strange as that related by Sir Arthur Conan Doyle in "The Lost World," and it has the advantage of being possible of verification. Brune, himself, is now making plans to equip a large exploring party and next spring he will go again into the Osage Hills determined to bring back concrete proof of his story.

The lost world, according to Brune, is located on a plateau about a mile high, the sides of which are so steep that it is impossible to climb them unassisted. He was alone when he found the plateau and was unable to scale the precipitous cliffs.

But what convinced him that animal life on the plateau was the same as that which existed several hundred years ago was the result of a hunting trip. Brune saw a bird, of strange appearance, and he shot it. He found that it had leather wings without feathers and that its mouth was furnished with a complete set of teeth. Altho he did not know that the bird answers to the name of pterodactyl in science, he did realize that it was a strange species.

So steep were the cliffs leading up to the plateau on all sides that the animals on the summit were unable to descend and the men below were so far away that they could not distinguish their characteristics except that they were different from all animals known to the huntsman.

So Brune decided to return to civilization and to get an outfit which would enable him and his friends to return to the Osage Hills, scale the cliffs of the mysterious plateau, and see it firsthand the mysteries of the life existing there.

The plateau is completely isolated from surrounding country. But Brune says that with the aid of ropes and plenty of men he believes the cliffs can be scaled.

Heavy rifles will be carried by the men making up the party and the expectation that they may meet with some of the great animals described in books devoted to prehistoric animal life.

Brune only talks of his experience to those who are intimate with him. He fears he will not be believed because of the strangeness of his story. But he swears he tells the truth and he is determined to prove the most cynical that the lost world really exists. He is determined to bring back to civilization specimens of strange animal life, carcasses and skins.

As if the homage to *The Lost World* wasn't bad enough, basically all the articles contained on page three of that particular paper were of a dubious nature. Other stories alongside this one included a 200-pound baby, a monster greenback frog, and a 127-year-old Native American man to list only a few. That all said, *The Lost World* was itself based upon potentially true reports of isolated plateaus and prehistoric monsters loose in South America. Furthermore, there was even an isolated plateau explored in the Grand Canyon around this same time in hopes not of finding dinosaurs, but a race of prehistoric pygmy horses.

BY BEN E. TITUS.
United Press Staff Correspondent.

Portland, Ore., Dec. 15.—A section of the Columbia glacier, which had broken off and was found floating in Prince William Sound off the Alaskan coast, may reveal to scientists some of the secrets of prehistoric life before the glacial period.

Imbedded in the fragment of glacier was the skeleton of a huge monster, with some pieces of flesh still preserved by the action of the cold.

It was found by Jerry O'Leary and Charles Gibson, fishermen, who towed their find to port.

The skeleton measured 26 feet long, from head to tail, and was 39 inches wide. The head alone was about 55 inches in length. The center vertebra was 7 inches long, the top blades 14 inches, and the flippers 40 by 8 inches. The estimated weight of the monster was 1000 pounds. An official investigating party has left for Cordova to inspect the skeleton.

Likelihood that the skeleton may actually be that of some hitherto known prehistoric mammal is seen in recent geological discoveries in northern waters.

It has been found that the Japanese current, sweeping into the north coast of British Columbia and Alaska, has eaten away the glaciers in that region, and thus revealing many new signs of the life existing before the glacial period.

Some of these finds may have dated back to the Pleneolithic age, it is thought.

Chehalis Bee Nugget (December 19, 1930).

THE GLACIER MONSTER
Enigma From Alaska

THE FOLLOWING STORY has garnered a somewhat dubious reputation in the annals of cryptozoology. Published back in 1930, it was for a time taken fairly seriously until what appeared to be variations of the same article reappeared several times over the next few decades. As such, the original story was labeled as a hoax. But was it really?

Here's what we know: On November 10, 1930, two Alaskan men, Jerry O'Leary, a fox farmer, and his employee, Charles Gibson, sighted a large carcass trapped within a glacier floating through the waters of Prince William Sound. The two had been making their usual rounds to feed the foxes when Gibson spotted the remains of a huge creature within a block of ice washed up on the Columbia Glacier, six miles north of them.

Illustration from one of the articles, date unknown.

The two men hooked the carcass and arduously brought it all the way onto shore. Afterwards, they cut off some of the mystery animal's flesh, which they described as resembling and smelling like horse meat. They hung it in the smoke house to later use as feed for some foxes on the farm.

News of the discovery reached the settlements of Valdez and Cordova. Eventually, the story caught the ear of Charles Flory of the U.S. Forest Service and W.J. McDonald, the district forest supervisor of the Chugach National Forest. Flory and McDonald mounted an expedition to inspect the carcass themselves along with Captain E.N. Jacobson, Lee C. Pratt, John V. Lydick, Howard W. Stewart, and A.C. Faith on November 25th.

It was also on the 25th that articles on the creature began appearing in the papers. This one was published in the Washington D.C. *Evening Star* on November 25, 1930, and appeared to be unaware of the McDonald expedition already in progress:

CARCASS OF LIZARDLIKE ANIMAL, 42 FEET LONG, FOUND IN ALASKA.
Strange Creature, With Fur in Perfect Condition, Incased in Ice of Columbia Glacier.

By the Associated Press.
CORDOVA, Alaska, November 25. - Reports received from Valdez today said the carcass of a giant lizardlike creature, with fur in perfect condition, had been found on Glacier Island, near here.

The strange creature reported to be 42 feet long, including a tail measuring 16 feet, was believed to have been preserved since prehistoric times by being incased in ice in the upper reaches of the Columbia Glacier. The ice was believed to have worked its way gradually to the sea. The head was reported to be 6 feet long and the body 20 feet in length.

NEW YORK. November 25 (AP). - Bernard Brown, curator of the American Museum of Natural History, has requested Dr. Charles E. Bunnell, president of Alaska College at Fairbanks, to investigate the carcass of the strange creature found on Glacier Island.

The museum was informed of the supposed find 10 days ago.

"So far as we know," said Mr. Brown, "there was no prehistoric creature of the dimensions given in the dispatch from Alaska.

"If the creature was incased in ice it must have lived when the ice was formed. The prehistoric animals of Alaska of which we know were the mammoth and the buffalo and many small creatures, none of which would reach the dimensions of the lizardlike animal.

"The description suggests a reptile something like a dinosaur, but dinosaurs died out millions of years before the ice age. The only other possibility is that it is some sort of a marine creature like a whale."

Mr. Brown does not expect a report from Dr. Bunnell for some time because of the difficulty of making a Winter journey from Fairbanks to Glacier Island.

Did Dr. Bunnell ever make the journey to Glacier Island to inspect the carcass for himself? That's hard to say, but Bunnell was at least real. In addition to being the president of Alaska College at that time, he had also served as a district judge for the United States Fourth Judicial Division between 1915-1922. In any case, Bunnell needn't have worried, as W.J. McDonald would eventually make a thorough study of the body.

Portrait photograph of Charles E. Bunnell during his term as a judge of the United States territorial court for the Territory of Alaska.

An article appeared in none other than *TIME Magazine* on December 8, 1930, on the creature, comparing it to the recent phenomenon of Ogopogo, British Columbia's lake monster. It updated the proceedings and disclosed that W. J. McDonald had confirmed the discovery. Despite earlier reports that made it much larger, McDonald found that the creature was only 24 feet long. There was no fur on the body, and he, too, likened it to a huge lizard with a long tail and tapering head. The snout, he said, resembled a pelican's beak. The head, however, he said was elephant-like. It was reported that six feet worth of flesh had been preserved, but foxes and sled dogs had eaten the rest. The article ended by revealing that the carcass was taken to Cordova, and as soon as the weather would permit, Dr. Bunnell would go to Cordova to see it for himself.

Cryptopia produced a well-done article on the carcass in recent years that dredged up some alternate quotes worth printing, such as McDonald stating that "The (creature) had a long tail and tapering head, much like a dinosaur."[21] McDonald's measurements of the creature were as follows: the elephant-like head was 59 inches long, while the trunk or snout was 39 inches from the center of the forehead and was 11 inches wide at the midsection with a 29-inch circumference overall. The widest part of the body overall measured 38 inches across at 24 feet long. The tail, which started at the rib section, was said to be

---

21 https://www.cryptopia.us/site/2010/01/glacier-island-carcass-alaska-usa/

14 feet. As to the overall weight, McDonald estimated it at 1,000 pounds. Like the carcass's discoverers, O'Leary and Gibson, McDonald described the flesh as horse-like. As for other odd details, the head attached directly to the torso with no visible neck according to some sources. Most interesting of all, the carcass was said to possess flippers that were measured at three feet eleven inches in length and eight inches wide. According to some reports, after this, the body drifted back into the ocean never to be seen again.

Elephantine Sea Monster.

For many years thereafter, cryptozoologists wondered just what the creature could have been. Some compared it to Trunko, a 1922 carcass that washed ashore on a South African beach. Trunko was named such because it had a trunk and could only be described as an aquatic mastodon as odd as that may sound. Other researchers likened the Glacier Island carcass to the Hoarde Monster of

Adelaide, Australia, discovered by Mr. Hoarde in September of 1883. Charles Fort reported on it in *Lo!*, and considered it so strange in appearance he half-joked that it may have come from another planet:

> Remains of a strange animal, teleported to this earth from Mars or the moon—very likely, or not so likely—found on a bank of a stream in Australia. See the *Adelaide Observer*, Sept. 15, 1883—that Mr. Hoad, of Adelaide, had found on a bank of Brungle Creek, a headless trunk of a pig-like animal, with an appendage that curved inward, like the tail of a lobster.

For years I was led to believe the 1930 account of the Glacier Island carcass was a hoax until I finally stumbled across a photograph of it during a newspaper search. There right in front of me appeared to be photographic proof that there was indeed a real carcass. Only it really didn't look like a dinosaur.

I was late to the party as it turned out. Karl Shuker and Loren Coleman had posted the truth about the skeleton's rather mundane nature some time back. The photograph was taken by Howard Stewart of the Associated Press and rather quickly, the skeleton was identified as that of a pike whale. Nor did the skeleton drift out to sea never to be seen again as is often reported. In truth, it was purchased for $600 not too long after its discovery in January of 1931 by Tom Vevig, who owned taxicab company. Despite its identification as a whale, Vevig began marketing it as "Alaska's Prehistoric Monster."

Scientists Believe Glacial Visitor May Be Prehistoric Monster Millions Of Years Old

From the *Chehalis Bee Nugget*
of December 19, 1930.

The plan was to mount the skeleton for display in Cordova and then move it elsewhere. By late February, *Vevig* and his wife had booked passage on the steamer Yukon to transport the skeleton to Seattle. There, the Vevigs hauled the skeleton by a truck that was specially outfitted to carry the skeleton. Advertisements screamed the following:

Alaska's Prehistoric Monster — Millions of years old. Nearly 30 feet long. Baffles the scientific world. Queerest monster ever found.

Discovered in Columbia Glacier. Now on Exhibit. Here for a short time. Don't miss it. 25 cents Adults, 15 cents, children any time.

> **Find Rare Whale.**
> CORDOVA, Alaska.—A rare example of a pike whale, thought to be millions of years old, was recently taken from glacier ice on Glacier Island near here. This prehistoric monster had the beak of a pelican and a head like an elephant. It measured 42 feet in length, including a 6-foot head and a 16-foot tail.

Ardmore Daily Ardmoreite (March 8, 1931).

By June of that same year, they reached Chicago, and by the end of the summer they had even managed to tour the skeleton through Mexico and parts of Canada in addition to the U.S.

The Vevigs were back home by September, where they reported that the tour had been a great success. After this, it was donated to the National Museum of Natural History in Washington, D.C. Today the skeleton still rests there in storage and was actually identified as the remains of a Northern Minke Whale rather than a Piek Whale.

Sources:

Coleman, Loren. "Alaska's Prehistoric Monster." CRYPTOZOONEWS (May 4, 2008)

Lambert, Dixie. "'Sea Monster' discovery on Glacier Island the buzz of old Cordova." *The Cordova Times* (May 02, 2008)

Morphy, Rob. "GLACIER ISLAND CARCASS: (ALASKA, USA)." Cryptopia. (January 14, 2010)
https://www.cryptopia.us/site/2010/01/glacier-island-carcass-alaska-usa/

Shuker, Karl. "Son of Trunko!" Karl Shuker Blogspot. (September 16, 2010)
http://karlshuker.blogspot.com/2010/09/son-of-trunko.html

SIDE STORY
The Continued Adventures of
the Glacier Island Carcass

Another reason as to why so many people wrote the Glacier Island story off as a complete fabrication—and not a simple misidentification of a whale carcass—was because the story was repurposed at least three times over the next thirty years. Or, at least, it appeared to have been. As it turned out, rather than the old article being repurposed three times, there were simply three more misidentified whale carcasses that washed ashore over the years, all three of which were very similar to the Glacier Island story. These new carcasses were dubbed "prehistoric monsters" as well. And perhaps one of them could have been? As you'll soon see, one of the articles hinted that the carcass in question wasn't a whale, but possibly an actual dinosaur this time.

The first article that I could find came from the *Centralia Evening Sentinel* of June 28, 1945:

DISCOVER REMAINS OF
PREHISTORIC MONSTER

CORDOVA. Alaska. June 28 IP —Residents of Katalla, 40 miles east of here, today were attempting to get some expert to identity the well preserved remains of a prehistoric monster, discovered by a trapper on a sandbar in the glacier-fed Tsivat river.

Tom White, longtime resident of Katalla, said Paul Schneurn told him he found a portion of a carcass, 12 feet long and six feet high, protruding from the sand-bar. Bears had been gnawing it, he added.

Only a year later yet another article appeared in *The Traverse City Record-Eagle* on October 25, 1946. However, this one does seem repetitive of the original story from 1930, hence the confusion:

Prehistoric Monster Found in Alaska

ANCHOR POINT, ALASKA, Oct. 2nd— (AP)— Anthropologists from the University of Alaska at Fairbanks were enroute here today to examine the body of a huge, lizard-like creature identified tentatively as a prehistoric tyrannosaurus or gorgonosaurus.

It was believed to have been preserved in a glacier until washed ashore here Wednesday. Although positive identification by experts has not yet been made, Fairbanks physicians studying anthropology texts said the "creature" was "definitely prehistoric" and "may belong to one of two species".

The creature measured nearly nineteen feet from tip to tail. Its head measured 2 feet by 2 ½ feet and its mouth featured a row of teeth 18 inches long.

"The animal had large hind legs and a heavy thigh bone which measured, approximately 4 feet from the hip to the first joint. The forelegs were short and heavy.

Leathery skin on the head and neck was covered with bristly hair and flesh almost completely covered the head, shoulders and hips. The backbone had broken through the animal's side and there was some evidence of decomposition".

Body of Prehistoric Monster Is Found

ANCHORAGE, Alaska, Oct. 24.—(U.P.)—Residents Wednesday believed the body of a huge fur-bearing lizzard-like creature washed ashore at Homer, Alaska, on Cook's inlet, was that of a prehistoric monster.

The mammal measured 18 feet 10 inches from the tip of its crocodile-shaped jaws to the end of the lizzard-like tail. The head was three and one-half feet long and two feet three inches wide. It had 22 lower teeth and 20 upper teeth, each about four inches in length.

Previously, at least three other "prehistoric" monsters have been found but investigation has proven the others to be whales.

Butte Montana Standard (October 25, 1946).

Though I initially brushed this off as a shameless repeat of the 1930 story, I came across an additional article, pictured above, from the *Butte Montana Standard* of October 25, 1946. It concluded its report by stating that "Previously, at least three other 'prehistoric' monsters have been found but investigation has proven the others to be whales." As such, the brief article would seem to imply that this carcass was possibly a real monster and not a whale. Or maybe they were just pulling their collective reader's legs.

Ten years later, on July 23, 1956, another carcass was reported in the *Oakland Tribune* with the following headline: "MONSTER: Huge Hairy Beast Lies On Beach". The story claimed that "The monstrous carcass was discovered on the beach 60 miles southeast of here two months; ago by Earl Flemming."

It also noted that "Conservative estimates place the size of the monster at more than 100 feet in length and 15 feet wide at its broadest visible point". Like the previous creatures, this one had hair in the form of two-inch-long reddish-brown bristles. Its teeth were reported as six inches long and five inches wide at the bottom. Its ribs, they said, extended from five to six feet from its spinal column.

This one, too, as it turned out, was another beaked whale as revealed in an article published in the July 26, 1956 *Fairbanks Daily News Miner*. The carcass was examined by Dr. Peter Tack of the University of Michigan and identified as a 38-foot-long beaked whale. As to the exaggerated reports that it was 100 feet, Tack observed that part of the monster's body was buried and obscured in sand, which may have led some early observers to become overly enthusiastic as to the creature's size.

Jersey Devil Footprints of 1909.

THE JERSEY DEVIL RIDES OUT
Winged Fiend Flies Again

DUE TO ITS UNIQUE appearance, the Jersey Devil has carved out quite a niche for itself in the annals of cryptozoology. As with any cryptid, descriptions of it vary, but in essence the creature is often described as either a winged biped or quadruped. It's often mammalian in appearance, sometimes being likened to a horse with wings, and it definitely has hooves if some accounts are to be believed. A few have tried to link it to remnant pterodactyls, as did one of the 1909 articles,[22] but if we're being honest, the Jersey Devil is definitely a whatisit.[23]

---

[22] Included in the appendix.

[23] Along the same lines as Texas's "Big Bird" flap of 1976, some have simply shrugged the Jersey Devil off as a large sandhill crane rather than a prehistoric monster.

In folklore, the creature is said to be the devilish offspring of the Leeds family. According to area lore, the in-humanoid beast was birthed of a human mother in the Pine Barrens. Back in 1735, a woman known simply as "Mother Leeds" who already had a dozen children was on the verge of begrudgingly birthing her 13th. In the midst of her labor pains on a stormy night, she cursed the child in frustration, declaring that it would be a devil. And then, according to legend, out popped a creature with a goat's head, hooves, bat wings, and a forked tail. The "child" then escaped through the chimney and became the flying Jersey Devil seen ever since.

Among those to sight the Jersey Devil in the early days were none other than Commodore

Stephen Decatur and even Napoleon's older brother, Joseph Bonaparte. By the 1840s, the Jersey Devil was routinely blamed for livestock killings. Though it had been seen off and on in the state of New Jersey since the 18th Century, its biggest flap ever occurred in the New Year of 1909.

Literally hundreds of sightings were recorded, and some were quite wild, with the monster attacking a trolley car in Haddon Heights and also a club in Camden. Fear grew to such heights that a few schools even closed down in the Delaware Valley and groups of hunters went out to shoot the monster down. Today the hundreds—some say thousands—of sightings are brushed off as a mere case of mass hysteria, but were they really?

From the best that I can tell, the 1909 flap began on the night of January 16th in Woodbury, New Jersey, when a man heard a strange hissing noise in the air as he departed a hotel. He looked above him to see a white object with glowing eyes flying over the street. "I saw two spots of phosphorus; the eyes of the beast. There was a white cloud, like escaping steam from an engine. It moved as fast as an auto," reported one paper.

On the 17th, E.W. Minster, the local postmaster, was also awakened by strange noises in Bristol at 2 A.M. The sound seemed to be coming from the direction of the Delaware River and struck him as supernatural. He peeked out his window towards the river and saw what appeared to be a large crane, only its body was luminescent just like the previous night's sighting.

BROAD AND COOPER STREET

His sighting was reported as follows:

Its head resembled that of a ram, with curled horns, and its long thick neck was thrust forward in flight. It had long thin wings and short legs, the front legs shorter than the hind. Again it uttered its mournful and awful call—a combination of a squawk and a whistle, the beginning very high and piercing and ending very low and hoarse.[24]

---

[24] Quoted in *Monsters You Never Heard Of*, pp.14-15.

TS, WOODBURY, NEW JERSEY

Around the same time, an entire trolley car's worth of passengers sighted the creature flying above them on their way from Clementon to Camden. Lewis Boeger, the conductor, was quoted in the papers with the following description:

In general appearance it resembled a kangaroo. It has a long neck and from what glimpse I got of its head its features were hideous. It has wings of a fairly good size and of course in the darkness looked black. Its legs

143

are long and somewhat slender and were held in just such a position as a swan's when it is flying. We all tried to get a look at its feet to see what shape they were but the darkness was too great. It looked to be about four feet high.[25]

The big event that really kicked off the Jersey Devil mania was a set of hoofprints found in the snow one morning. Over the next several days, the papers were packed with reports of the monster. As there are enough reports to fill a tome all their own, I will reprint only a select few. The following was published on January 20th and gives a good rundown on the mysterious hoofprints:

Hunting Expeditions Seek Strange Creature Which Has left Hoof-Like Tracks in Many Sections

BURLINGTON, N.J., Jan. 20.—Determined to trap, shoot or in some way determine the identity of the mysterious creature or creatures whose hoof-like tracks are to be seen today across almost any section of the surrounding rural regions, as well as across roofs, fences and back yards in practically every block in Burlington city, farmers today set out hundreds of steel traps where the uncanny tracks are most plainly marked in the snow, and tonight scores of young men, armed with shotguns, are

---

[25] Ibid, p.15.

watching for the strange beast that has thrown this section into a state bordering on panic.

Efforts of a party of young farmers living near Jacksonville to track the creature today proved fruitless. Hounds put on the trail refused to follow the tracks, and, with bristling hair and the picture of terror, ran home. The farmers followed the tracks for nearly four miles, when the hoof prints mysteriously disappeared.

May Be Lots of Them

The footprints of what many old residents believe is the "Leeds Devil," which was a real terror to lonely neighborhoods in bygone years, appear in practically every part of this city. If "devil" it is, then there must be a whole troupe of them, for the tracks in some places are big enough for a horse, yet lead through fence holes but two feet high, while at other places they are but two inches in diameter. In a yard in the rear of the store of Joseph Lowden the tracks lead under the shed and around the yard, and stop beside a garbage can, which was overturned and its contents partly devoured. At the home of Philip Gallagher the hoofmarks are on the roof of a shed, along a snow-covered fence top and even on a window ledge.

Residents in the colored section where the creature seems to have jumped fences and tramped about the yards in search of food, are panic stricken, and have their doors closely barricaded tonight. Old negroes say the creature is the "Flying Death" and their stories have not added to the peace of mind of their communities.

Many Sections Visited

Reports today from Woodbury and other sections state that the same tracks were seen there. It would have been impossible for one animal to have traversed the territory in one night. The mystery has been discussed among scientific men, one theory advanced is that during Saturday night's heavy snow storm several flocks of wild geese flew over this section, and becoming tired settled. Their web feet made an impression in the snow, which was flattened and made solid by the rain which followed. The steps are of about the distance these fowls would make, yet many persons knowing the habits of these fowl say that the birds would have made a tremendous noise aa they came down.

These tracks are all pointed going and coming from a chicken yard, or the rear of houses where garbage had emptied, showing that the fowl or animal was in search of something to eat.

A startling story comes from Gloucester, where it appears this "animal" was seen Sunday night. Nelson Evans, of 205 Mercer street, declares he and his wife were awakened about half past two o'clock in the morning by a noise on the shed roof. Getting up they saw a "bird" about three feet six inches high, with wings two feet and a half long, with a head like a collie and with a horse's face; a neck like a crane, four legs, the two front ones being short and that the bird flew away shortly after they saw it. The prints made in the snow at the Evans' house are similar to those seen else-where.

The tracks of the strange creature have been found today at Merchantville, Riverside, Collingswood and other South Jersey towns. At Riverside the creature killed a small dog in the yard of Joseph Manz's residence.

On the 22nd, it was reported that the creature had been seen in the West End and had a run-in with the law:

STRANGE CREATURE SEEN IN THE WEST END

it had wings like a bat and was chased by a squad of policemen.

The strange animal or bird which is terrorizing several sections of the city, made its appearance last night in the Tenth Ward. A respected citizen of that Ward, who resides at third and Jeffrey streets on his way home from the ninth Street trolley line at 1030 o'clock, had his attention attracted by strange noises on the roof of the sheds of Robinson's backyard.

Suddenly there was a floundering and struggling in the center of Engle Street, and out of the confusion there arose a strange-looking animal – half beast and half bird – with wings like a bat and a long tail, the end of which looked like the point of an arrow. The weather was very foggy, but the clear of the electric lights, the citizen saw the strange-looking animal fly down Engle Street. As it neared the elevated railroad it seemed to rise like a big airship, and passed over the tracks just as a northbound express train was passing.

Whether it be a beast or bird, it was of sufficient size to cause the engineer to sound a sharp danger signal from his whistle. The strange creature was next seen soaring over the top of the borough hall and alighted near the public school building at third and Jeffrey streets. At this point several of the police officers started in pursuit of the beast or bird, or whatever it is. They gave chase up Commerce Street to the rear of the undertaking establishment of Thomas Minshall, where the animal was lost in the fog. The tracks of the creature could be plainly followed in the snow and people living in the neighborhood say that they heard distinctly the rustle of wings and the clatter of strange feet at a late hour.

An examination revealed the fact that several of the telephone wires were torn down and it is supposed that this was done by the animal coming in contact with the cables during its flight.

J. Vernon Williams, roadmaster for Middletown Township is reported to have seen the "devil" or by whatever name one wishes to call the strange animal which made its appearance in the city a few days ago. Mr. Williams says that about 2 o'clock this morning he was awakened by the noises made by three dogs. Going to the window he observed the dogs running about a peculiar kind of animal, all apparently afraid to make an attack upon it. Mr. Williams is reported to have watched the actions of the dogs for some time and then decided to raise the window. As he did so the noise frightened off the strange appearing creature and all trace of it has been lost.

The saga of the flying devil died out by February but made a surprise resurgence at the end of the same summer. *The Bisbee Daily Review* of August 3, 1909, reported the following:

"Queer Creature Causes Alarm"

Devil Horse Roams About Frightening People In Vicinity Of Philadelphia.

Search Made By Armed Men

Hunt For Strange Animal That Makes Odd Footprints And Runs Through Deep Snow On Only Two Legs.

Philadelphia – Clearly defined in the crust of the snow, the footprints of a two-legged beast or bird, shod with steel, are creating a tremendous sensation in this city and the South Jersey towns. People who read this narrative may form their own opinions as to the cause of these manifestations.

It was originally intended to treat this subject with a light and scoffing touch; to make merry over the mystery of the "Leed's Devil" that has transformed scores of towns and hamlets of Camden, Gloucester and Burlington counties, into settlements of timid folk, where women and children fear to walk abroad at night, and armed men make nocturnal searches.

Before noon, however, the telephone wires were hot with messages from persons who had seen the hoofprints. Two men declared they had seen the marks in their own yards in this city. They were William L. Smith and William Heimbold, and their neighbors know them for sober truthful men.

Of course, practical people scoff at these reports, but none has yet offered an explanation that will meet the situation. Then comes Nelson Evans, a paper hanger of Gloucester City, with the declaration that he and his wife saw the "devil" early in the morning as he sat on the roof of their back shed.

White-faced and trembling, Evans entered police headquarters there the other morning and leaned up against the wall.

"I saw it," he whispered, round-eyed with recollection.

"You did!" exclaimed the chief. "What did it look like?"

"About two o'clock," said the paper hanger, "my wife and I were aroused by a noise on our shed roof. I went to the window and looked out and then I called her. We saw the strangest beast or bird, I don't know which, you ever heard of.

It was about three and a half feet high, with a head like a collie dog and a face like a horse. It had a long neck, wings about two feet long, and its back legs were like those of a crane, and it had horse's hoofs. It walked on its back legs and held up two short front legs with paws on them.

As far as I could tell, the thing seemed to be trying to get into the shed. My wife and I were scared, I tell you, but I managed to open the window and say 'Shoo!' and it turned around, barked at me, and then flew away."

The tracks were first seen after the heavy snowfall, but at first nothing was said about them, as they were believed to be the work of some practical joker. Then it was noticed that

151

the mysterious creature left hoof prints in farm yards and on roofs of buildings as well.

Marks of the beast were found in Gloucester, Mount Holly, Clayton, Woodbury, Wenonah, Mantua, Paulsboro, Lumberton, Ayerstown, Vincetown, Almonessen, Mount Ephraim, and other towns within a radius of twenty miles or more. This nearly upset the theory that it was the work of a joker and the oldest inhabitant got busy.

He remembered that as far back as 1869 that part of South Jersey was visited by a creature that was known as "Leed's Devil," because it was supposed to emerge from Leed's point, on Brigantine beach. The "devil" reappeared in 1874 and 1879 and even as recently as 1904.

Early in the morning there came a report that the monstrosity had crossed the river and was disporting himself in the yards of residents of Sansom street, above Forty-fifth street.

A young man who gave his name as Harry L. Smith, said that in the yard of his home there were marks like the footprints of a two-legged horse.

That was all of the summer monster flap, if it could even be called that. However, the tale of the devil wasn't over yet, and appeared to conclude that fall. By October, reports surfaced that the beast was dead. This version comes from the November 10, 1909, edition of *The Citizen,* which reported,

DEAD 'JERSEY DEVIL' FOUND IN WOODS.

Body of Strange Animal Explains Puzzling Hoofprints Left in the Snow.

SENT TO THE STATE MUSEUM.
The Spinal Column Extends Six Inches Behind Junction with Hind Legs, Somewhat After the Manner of the Tail of a Kangaroo.

Burlington, N.J. - If anybody ever doubted that a "Jersey Devil" left its strange and puzzling hoofprints in the snow of this and adjoining States last winter, proof was produced here that the scare was never due to highballs. There is on exhibit in this city the carcass of the queerest animal ever seen about here, a beast not on the schedule of any natural history ever read by any one of this section.

The animal's body, still in good condition, as though it had been dead only a short while, was found by Morris Cabinsky of this city, and Charles Malsbury of Kinkora, in the woods near Kinkora, and was brought to this city, where hundreds have seen and marveled. Photographs have been made of the beast and Prof. Henry Morse, curator of the State Museum, will be asked to give the animal a name and place it where it belongs - if he is able to do so.

The boys thought at first they had come upon the carcass of a big wildcat, but it looked so queer to them that they decided to carry it into town.

The body of the animal is about twenty inches long and thin. The spinal column extends six inches behind the junction with the hind legs like the tail of a kangaroo, but this again is tipped with nine inches of tail like a squirrel's, but of reddish-brown fur. The strangest feature of all and that which would seem to convict it of last winter's famous hoofprints, is found in the fore legs and feet. The legs are fifteen inches long, consisting of four joins and socketed to these are feet, which take the form of a broad, flat bone with a distinct heel. The foot bones are two and a half inches long and over and inch broad in a solid piece.

If the animal traveled by leaps bending the two fore feet down together, he would land after each long spring with the feet forming the puzzling effect of the hoofprints in the snow last winter. The rear feet would explain the finding of "cat" prints near the hoof marks. What looks like the framework of a pair of short wings rises from the animal's back, just above its short hind legs.

The big mouth is set with sharp teeth three quarters of an inch long, while the head is adorned with long, lance-like ears and whiskers four inches long.

This body would later be revealed to be a hoax—

more on that later. That said, naturally this wasn't the end of the devil. It reappeared only to "die" again in December of 1925 in Greenwich. There a farmer shot it dead as it was attacking his chickens. Supposedly, he photographed the body and showed it to hundreds of people, none of which could identify it. Of course, no one has seen said photo recently. Despite its numerous deaths, sightings continue on to this day. However, none of those sightings have compared to the 1909 flap.

9TH AND ARCH MUSEUM

T. F. HOPKINS   Manager

CAUGHT!!!
AND HERE!!!
ALIVE!!!
THE

LEEDS DEVIL
Captured Friday After a
Terrific Struggle

EXHIBITED EXCLUSIVELY HERE AT
9:00:00 A WEEK
The Fearful, Frightful,
Ferocious Monster Which
Has Been Terrorizing
Two States

Swims! Flys! Gallops!
Exhibited Securely Chained
In a Massive Steel Cage

A LIVING DRAGON
More Ferocious Than
the Fabled Monster
of Mythology
DON'T MISS THE
SIGHT OF A LIFETIME.

BIG STRING OF
SENSATIONS IN
CURIO HALL

THEATRE
GRAND CONTINUOUS VAUDEVILLE

10c ADMITS TO ALL

According to some, it was the publicist for Philadelphia's Arch Street Museum, Norman Jeffries, who began circulating the 1909 stories when the museum proprietor, T. F. Hopkins, claimed that the museum was in danger of closing unless they could boost attendance.

Jeffries then summoned the Jersey Devil to do his bidding via what many claim were fake stories. An article in the *Evening Journal* on January 22, 1909, was particularly damning, as it put forth the theory that the animal had only one leg due to the nature of the lone hoofprints in the snow. Unfortunately, this would seem to lend credence to the theory that it was all a hoax.

But can all of them really be fake? For certain, Jeffries did conspire with an animal trainer friend, Jacob Hope, to procure a kangaroo from a circus which they glued artificial claws and bat wings onto. They exhibited it at the museum, it was a success, and later in the 1920s, Jeffries finally admitted to his mischievous scheme.

On the one hand, it does seem easy to explain away the 1909 Jersey Devil flap as being created solely by Jeffries. Once the papers worked the public into a frenzy, perhaps some witnesses did observe a sandhill crane and got carried away. But what about some of the other accounts? How do we know for certain which were fabricated and which may have been genuine? Furthermore, what about all the sightings that pre-dated the 1909 flap and those that continued after? Though the 1909 chapter in the saga of the Jersey Devil is a nefarious one, it's still not enough to kill one of cryptozoology's favorite cryptids.

Sources:

Cohen, Daniel. *Monsters You Never Heard Of.* Dodd, Mead & Company, 1980.

THE CARLSBAD CREATURE
Dinosaur in the Hills

LIVING IN THE LAND OF ALIENS—that being Roswell, New Mexico—it's always a thrill for me when I can discover a dino-encounter close to home rather than another UFO sighting. In this case, close to home would be Carlsbad, New Mexico, a little less than 100 miles from the Alien City. Carlsbad, of course, is most famous for the Carlsbad Caverns, one of the best-known tourist attractions in New Mexico.

The massive cave system was discovered in 1898 by Jim White, and by 1923 it was declared a National Monument by President Calvin Coolidge. By the early 1930s it was a State Park, and from there grew into a major tourist destination.

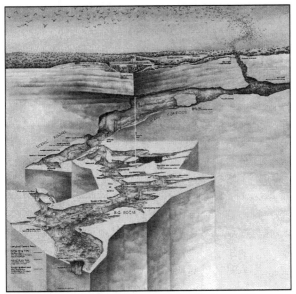

Map of Carlsbad Caverns by Robert Hynes
(National Park Service).

While I would love to be able to tie the following story into the cave system, or to be able to believe it all for that matter, there's sadly not much that I can say about the tale. It was printed in the July 6, 1948 issue of the Carlsbad *Daily Current-Argus*, which had recently urged readers to send letters telling of strange occurrences. A few had written in accounts of a headless horseman in the area, and some had also jokingly written in about a "horseless headman" in turn. Fowler Merritt, being much more original, wrote in with this dinosaur account, which he stated took place in the late 1930s. With no further ado, Fowler's letter:

Ramon Faulk stands before his little service station in Happy Valley, New Mexico in the vicinity of where the alleged sighting took place.
(NearLovingsBend.com 1938.095)

I do not want to alarm anyone or to cause undue apprehension, but I honestly think there is a real menace in the hills west of Carlsbad. About ten years ago I was out in the flats at the base of the hills west of Happy Valley. I had my little son and a dog with me. I had a .12 gauge shotgun, pump, and a .45 Colt automatic.

Just before dark a horrible thing rushed out of a deep canyon toward the boy and the dog who had strayed off to one side as boys do. I was almost paralyzed but the boy streaked toward me.

The dog stood his ground but his terror was pitiful. This apparition, or whatever, had the body of a good-sized horse and the head of a snake on a long neck. The head was stretched out toward my boy and the drumming of the animal's feet and the screams of the boy and the frantic barking of the dog kept me frozen.

I did manage to pump several loads of bird shot into the thing at rather long range and it slowed down. My boy got to me and behind me and then the thing seemed to notice the dog. Its long neck stretched out with this nasty head on the end of it and the jaws grabbed the dog. As it wheeled and started back into the canyon I grabbed the .45 and emptied it at the thing's head. I know some of the shots took effect but some missed. Our heroic dog was carried away before our eyes and we were afraid to follow. I was thankful that the boy escaped, but he was sick with brain fever for weeks. Even now, a grown man with the battles of the Pacific behind him, he won't talk of this and he refuses to go past Happy Valley.

You may laugh at the Headless Horseman or the Horseless Headsman if you wish; it is no joke to me, I assure you.

I inquired as to the identity of Fowler Merrit and could find no record of him living in Carlsbad. This proves nothing one way or the other, but it's discouraging, nonetheless. Was Fowler serious in his closing statement about this being a true encounter, or was it merely a wink and a nod at the reader? We will likely never know.

SIDE STORY
THE HOPPER WHOPPERS

The decade of the Great Depression was notorious for hoaxed photos of giant animals, and it would be a shame to leave out the saga of the "Hopper Whoppers". By the 1930s, photographers had mastered the art of photo manipulation, often via combining a wide shot and a close shot. The close shot would often be glued over the wide shot to create the fake. Then, one day, a man had the ingenious idea to have some fun with grasshoppers and photography.

It was Frank D. "Pop" Conrad of Garden City, Kansas, who created the postcards, or what he referred to as "hooper whoppers". Conrad explained that:

> The idea came to me after a flight of grasshoppers swarmed into Garden City attracted by the lights, and it was impossible to fill an automobile gasoline tank at filling

stations that night. I went home to sleep, but awoke at 3:00 a.m. and all I could think about was grasshoppers. By morning I had the idea of having fun with the grasshoppers, and took my pictures and superimposed the hoppers with humans. I didn't do it for adverse impressions of Kansas, but as an exaggerated joke.[26]

---

[26] https://www.kshs.org/kansapedia/exaggerated-postcards/10137

11

THE BEAR HYENA
Animal or Were-Beast?

EVERY SO OFTEN comes a one-off cryptid that is extremely hard to identify, as it matches nothing on record. The article below presents one such cryptid and was published sometime in February of 1929, though I have since lost the exact date of publication and the name of the newspaper:

PRESENCE OF HUGE BLACK BEAST STIRS TERROR NEAR NEW ALBANY

Farmer Surprises Monster Carrying Off Sixty Pound Pig, But Hairy Intruder Makes Escape Before Man Can Secure Gun

MYSTERIOUS BEAST OBJECT OF MAN HUNT

MYSTERIOUS ANIMAL SURPRISED IN BARNYARD NEAR GALENA BY YOUNG FARMER — FLEES WITH PIG

DOG PREVENTS ATTACK ON MAN

Canvass To Be Made Of All Zoos and Circuses in Southern Indiana— Tall Black Beast

GALENA, Ind., Feb. 6— Another hunt was to be started here today for the mysterious black beast that raided the A. A. Akins farm just east of here late yesterday, killed one pig and carried off in its "arms" another pig weighing 60 pounds, according to Leonard Akins, 20, who surprised the animal and was forced to flee for his life.

Posse of farmers aided by dogs, which tried to trail the black animal, failed to find it and returned last night still in doubt as to the identity of the creature.

"I can't imagine what it was unless it was a cross between a big bear and a hyena," young Akins said.

The hunters found one set of tracks that resembled bear tracks, Akins related, but as no one in the party was an expert on bears, the question was left open he said.

The alarm was given by Leonard Adkins, 20, who lives just east of Galena. Leonard walked into the barn and found the beast killing a 50-pound pig.

Dog Saves His Life.

The strange creature reared up on its hind legs as it caught sight of the youth and would have attacked him but Leonard's big air-dale dog dashed forward, and barked at it and the beast turned on the dog.

With the whole barnyard in an uproar Leonard sprinted back into the house to get a gun. He turned back just in time to see the animal pick up a 60-pound pig and start over a fence with it toward some woods.

"The animal was as large as a man and perfectly black," Leonard said. "It looked more like a hyena than anything I could compare it with."

The pig carried off by the animal was found about 100 yards from the barn torn to pieces.

Leonard's neighbors immediately joined in the hunt and this afternoon nearly every farmer in this vicinity was trailing the strange animal.

Galena is about eight miles north of New Albany.

It was thought possible that the beast might have escaped from some circus or zoo.

A variation of the article published around the same time was basically the same but with a few alterations and additional bits of information. I felt it was important because this article confirmed that the creature could take a bipedal stance. Headlined "MYSTERIOUS BEAST OBJECT OF MAN HUNT" and published in the *Greencastle Herald* on February 7, 1929, on page three, it reported additionally that:

The hunters found one tracks that resembled a bear's, Akins related but as no one-party was an expert on bears the question was left open he said.

"The critter walked on its hind legs, tail pointed ears, and ferocious teeth, I can say that much," Akins declared.

...

"The creature reared up on its hind legs and started toward me," Akins said. "My Airdale dog, however, dashed ahead and barked at it and it turned at the dog."

Akins then started to run to his home to get his gun. In running he glanced around and saw the animal seize another pig, which weighed at least 60 pounds, and take it in its "arms" to go across the fence and start for some woods.

"It was as big as a man and walked on its hind legs," the youth asserted.

A canvass will be made of all circuses and zoos in Southern Indiana to determine if any wild beast escaped.

As to what this beast was, the bipedal stance greatly complicates things. If not for that, one might could assume that it was a Bear Dog. Despite its name, bear dogs are not closely related to either of their namesakes, instead hailing from an extinct family of terrestrial carnivorans known as the *Amphicyonidae* of the suborder *Caniformia*. But, that said, they looked like a large variety of wolf crossed with a bear.

The fact that it used its arms to carry off its prey further complicates matters. As it stands, it would almost seem to sound more like a shapeshifter or, for lack of a better word, a type of werewolf! Like the Beast of Bladenboro which would come after, the creature's true identity will likely always remain a mystery.

SIDE STORY
Another Prehistoric Survivor Outside of Tombstone?

Any reader of this series will no doubt also be a fan of the Tombstone Thunderbird tale of 1890. In this case, here is another prehistoric beastie from the Huachuca Mountains, though lesser known. Unfortunately, I misplaced the exact date and paper, but I do recall that it came from sometime between 1900 to the early 1920s.

REPORT STRANGE ANIMAL FOUND IN THE HUACHUCAS

TOMBSTONE — That a strange species of animal appearing to be a cross between a bear and a lion has made its appearance in the Huachucas, is word received from J.H. Merritt, an old time pioneer, who has a ranch on the west side of the mountains. The animal, according to Mr. Merritt, is built like a bear and has feet like a bear, but his tail has the appearance of a lion, while his tusks are much larger than a bear's.

The animal attacked his dog and almost killed him before Mr. Meritt could dispatch him with a well directed shot. Describing the mysterious beast, Mr. Merrit in his letter received here by a friend:

"My dog treed a wild animal and I killed it. There is no one in the canyon who knows what it is. I never saw anything like it before.

It jumped out of the tree and my dog tied into, and I thought it would kill my dog before I could kill it.

"I have his hide here. He is built like a bear and has a foot like one, but has a tail as long as a lion's and I never saw such tusks as he had. He got my dog by the jaw and surely did hang on until the dog was almost breathless."

About a month ago Alf Bond reported seeing a strange animal in the Huachucas, and it may have been another like Mr. Meritt's find.

HOOSIER HUNTS 500-POUND TURTLE

Farmer Says Monster Reptile Lurks in Lake

CHURUBUSCO, Ind., March 10. (UP) Farmer Gale Harris sought the aid of an expert diver today to help him capture Oscar, the monster turtle of Fulks Lake.

Harris had a theory. He thought the diver could find the monster, pump it full of air, and float it to the surface.

Many people hereabouts, including Harris and members of his family, claim to have seen the giant reptile. They said it looks like an overgrown snapper weighing 400 to 500 pounds and with a head the size of a year-old baby.

Dozens of people flocked to the seven-acre lake on Harris' farm for a try at capturing Oscar.

Some used chicken wire stretched between fence posts as extra-strength seines while they criss-crossed the lake in boats. Helpers stood ready on shore with ropes to haul Oscar onto land if the hunters in the boats trapped him.

"We had him trapped in a net Saturday but he slithered away to one side and dove down into the water," Harris said. "I think a diver would be able to get him."

He denied a report that the turtle had come out of the lake and dragged several head of cattle into the 90-foot depths. He said, "The turtle's never been out of the lake, far as we know."

The hunters trying to capture Oscar were spurred by reports that the Cincinnati Zoo had offered $1800 for him—alive. Harris' wife said two investigators from the zoo came to verify that the turtle was in the lake.

"I don't know whether they saw it," she said, "but they seemed satisfied."

She said her brother, Charley Wilson, first saw the turtle swimming in the lake last summer. It disappeared from view until recently when Harris and their son, Vaughn, 12, spotted it again. She said Wilson's son-in-law also had seen it.

Harris said snapping turtles in these parts seldom grow to more than 14 to 15 pounds.

Clifford H. Pope, curator of reptiles at Chicago Museum of Natural History, said the record weight for a snapper is 86 pounds. He said only an alligator turtle from the south could weigh even as much as 200 pounds.

Pope doubted that Oscar had come that far.

Long Beach Press Telegram (March 10, 1949).

THE BUSCO BEAST
Oscar, the Titanic Turtle

CHURUBUSCO is a rural community of about 1,800 people located northwest of Fort Wayne, Indiana.[27] The town of Churubusco, like so many others, would go unnoticed by the rest of the world until something strange happened there. That strange something was the town's curious exploits to capture a giant turtle said to live in a lake there, which was covered in newspapers across the U.S. and even some in Europe in 1949.

---

[27] The town got its name from the Mexican-American War when the Americans won a victory in Churubusco, Mexico, on August 20, 1847. Ironically, before Churubusco was ever home to the giant turtle, it was also home to an Amerindian chieftain Little Turtle who headed the Miami Indian tribe and had met with three U.S. Presidents; George Washington, John Adams, and Thomas Jefferson.

Illustration by Neil Riebe.

It all started back in 1898 when Oscar Fulk claimed to see a gigantic turtle in a seven-acre lake located within his farmland. Another sighting followed in 1914, and after that, reports of the gigantic turtle were mostly forgotten. Fifty years after the original sighting, in July of 1948, two men were fishing on Fulk Lake, now owned by Gale Harris, when they, too, saw the giant turtle. Or so legend says. Some say that the two men, Ora Blue and Charley Wilson, actually faked the sighting based on the old stories of Oscar Fulk. Hoax or not, shortly after this, Harris himself saw the turtle, which was even bigger than what the two fishermen had claimed.

To prove that his sighting was genuine, Harris and some of the townspeople tried to capture the animal with a trap of stakes and chicken wire in a section of 10-foot-deep water. Rumor has it they almost did catch the turtle and a reel of film was taken of the event but it has since vanished. Churubusco's town paper reported on the capture attempts, which were then picked up by reporters in Ft. Wayne who sent the story across the wires on March 9, 1949.

It would be the Fort Wayne papers that jokingly named the turtle Oscar, after the lake's original owner, Oscar Fulk. Although the media was poking fun at Churubusco, the town's people took it very seriously and intensified their search—and they would not be alone. By March 14th, 3,000 visitors, a percentage of them media people, descended on Fulk Lake to watch the antics. Reports even say that there was bumper-to-bumper traffic in the town in addition to airplanes flying overhead.

The next attempt to find Oscar was the brainchild of Harris and a local mechanic, Kenneth Leitch. The two had engineered a sort of reverse periscope that Harris used to look underneath the water for Oscar. Later, divers would join in the search along the lake bottom, but difficulties with the suits, including a leaking helmet and sinking into the lake's murky bottom, caused problems. Still, the hunt persisted throughout the spring with all the zest of a *Looney Tunes* short, with Harris dropping dynamite into the water to bring Oscar to the surface and even releasing a female sea turtle in the lake to lure Oscar out (assuming that he was a male).

May Get Giant Turtle By Night

CHURUBUSCO, Ind., March 17 (UP)—Farmer Gale Harris said today that Oscar, the giant turtle of Fulks Lake, will be in captivity by nightfall "barring unforeseen difficulties."

Woodrow Rigsby, Fort Wayne, Ind., was ready to go down into the seven-acre lake in a reinforced diving suit to try to capture the monster.

Harris said he will be glad when the reptile is hauled out.

"I'm getting tired of people calling me a liar," he said. "I want to get the thing out of the lake and let the people see for themselves how big it is."

Some people who have seen the turtle claim it weighs a quarter of a ton. Naturalists doubt if it could be that large and Harris himself says it is somewhat smaller.

Thousands of sightseers have flocked to the Harris farm since the hunt for Oscar began two weeks ago.

Greencastle Daily Banner (March 17, 1949).

After all these attempts failed, it was down to the final straw: Harris was going to drain the lake until there was nowhere left for the titanic turtle to hide.

While this was occurring in September of 1949, the crowds that had begun to wane returned to watch this last-ditch effort to find Oscar. This time, though, Harris wisely charged the crowds to watch the process, which helped to pay for the draining of the lake.

Even as the lake began to shrink with the massive amounts of water being pumped out of it, Oscar still could not be found. And, just when Harris was getting to the end of his quest to bring Oscar to the surface, he was struck with appendicitis. By the time Harris got out of the hospital the lake had refilled with rainwater and Harris was financially ruined according to some. The search was officially over and Oscar would never resurface, leaving town residents to debate his existence. As for Harris, he left Churubusco.

I first read this story in Daniel Cohen's *Encyclopedia of Monsters* and was very intrigued by it. As such, I am now pleased to present to you some of the original newspaper accounts detailing the wild efforts to capture Oscar, starting with the *Greencastle Daily Banner* of March 11, 1949:

HIRES AIRPLANE TO
HUNT GIANT TURTLE

CHURUBUSCO, Ind., March 11 (UP) Farmer Gale Harris was busy welding a big cage today so he can exhibit Oscar, the giant turtle, when and if the reptile is captured and hauled out of Fulks Lake.

Harris hired an airplane to help in the search for the turtle rumored to be 500 years old and weigh 500 pounds. But bad weather temporarily halted the flight and Harris and his father-in-law Kenneth Leitch, started to build the cage.

The Cincinnati zoo denied that it would buy the turtle for $1,800, and called the report "absurd."

"We wouldn't pay $1,800 for any turtle. Not oven a performing one," zoo officials said.

But Harris was not disturbed. He said the hunt would continue anyway.

"The people are aroused now," he said. "They want to see that turtle."

Besides, he added with a grin, he probably could make $1,800 in less than a week by exhibiting the turtle.

The Fort Madison *Evening Democrat* reported on March 19, 1949, that:

CHURUBUSCO, Ind., (UP) — Gale Harris' crew of turtle trappers denied today that they were ready to give up the fight to capture Oscar, the giant turtle of Fulks Lake.

"This definitely is not the time for us to lose faith," Harris said. "We're going out today and bring him back alive."

Diver Woodrow Rigsby was all set to go into the seven-acre pond yesterday in search of Oscar when he discovered that his diving suit had sprung a leak.

The hunt had to be postponed while Rigsby repaired his equipment.

The suit was the second one sent from Chicago this week as Harris attempted to capture the turtle, sighted by several residents who claim he is 500 years old and weighs a quarter of a ton.

The *South Haven Daily Tribune* reported on May 23, 1949, the most humorous effort yet to capture Oscar (I assume the soup part is just a joke):

Tillie Turtle Fails, She's Just Soup Today

CHURUBUSCO. Ind. [UP] Tillie, a buxom lady turtle, failed to lure Oscar, the turtle giant of Fulk Lake, so she was soup today.

Divers tried to trap Oscar with love after trying vainly for months to get him out of the lake and onto scales. He reportedly weighs 500 pounds and is farmer Gale Harris claims, the biggest in these parts.

Harris owns Fulks Lake, where Oscar lives.

Charles Rayhill of Hunterstown, Ind., brought Tillie, a 225-pounder, from Key West, Fla. Walter Johnson of Chesterton, Ind, one of the divers, tied a rope around her and let her stroll around the lake bottom.

A jug tied to the rope floated, on the lake, to show Tillies position in her wooing of Oscar.

Either turtles don't fall in love fast or Tillie didn't run into Oscar.

Two days of waiting exhausted the patience of the watchers so they pulled Tillie out and made soup out of her.

Harris, however, is thinking about another possibility.

Maybe Oscar isn't a gentleman turtle after all.

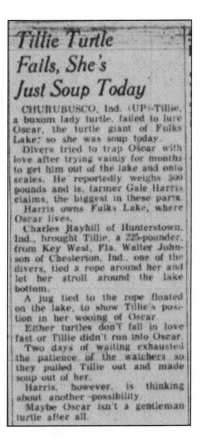

Tillie Turtle Fails, She's Just Soup Today

CHURUBUSCO, Ind. (UP)—Tillie, a buxom lady turtle, failed to lure Oscar, the turtle giant of Fulks Lake, so she was soup today.

Divers tried to trap Oscar with love after trying vainly for months to get him out of the lake and onto scales. He reportedly weighs 500 pounds and is, farmer Gale Harris claims, the biggest in these parts.

Harris owns Fulks Lake, where Oscar lives.

Charles Rayhill of Hunterstown, Ind., brought Tillie, a 225-pounder, from Key West, Fla. Walter Johnson of Chesterton, Ind., one of the divers, tied a rope around her and let her stroll around the lake bottom.

A jug tied to the rope floated on the lake, to show Tillie's position in her wooing of Oscar.

Either turtles don't fall in love fast or Tillie didn't run into Oscar.

Two days of waiting exhausted the patience of the watchers so they pulled Tillie out and made soup out of her.

Harris, however, is thinking about another possibility.

Maybe Oscar isn't a gentleman turtle after all.

The *Pocatello Post* of September 15, 1949, reported:

Oscar, Giant Turtle, May Lose This Round

CHURABUSCO, Ind. — (UP) —Oscar, the gigantic turtle who has outwitted every attempt by farmer Gale Harris to capture him, may lose his freedom to a gasoline driven pump.

Harris set the pump to draining the seven-acre Fulks Lake where Oscar lives. Harris figures that once the lake is dry it will be no trick at all to cage the turtle and haul him away.

No one has ever gotten a really good look at Oscar. But Harris claims that he weighs about 500 pounds and is at least a half century old.

Harris came closest to capturing the turtle when he and some neighbors put two electrodes into the lake and sent 2,500 volts through them.

Stunned fish, frogs, and Oscar floated to the surface but before the capture could be completed the wily turtle came to and paddled back to the muddy lake bottom.

In another attempt, Harris staked out a 150 pound female turtle to the lake shore but Oscar never even winked at her.

Nets, cages, and even divers yielded no better results. All this took a lot of time and Harris' farm work suffered. But the capture became an obsession with him and he secured permission from the Indiana conservation commission to drain the lake into another lake five miles away via drainage ditches.

"I want to show up the people who've called me a liar," he said.

The *Defiance Crescent News* of October 7, 1949, reported:

Indiana Governor Offers To Help Churubusco Farmer Capture Turtle

Churubusco, Ind., Oct. 7—Farmer Gale Harris, the man who has been hunting a 300-pound turtle in his farm pond near Churubusco, since last spring, was back at it again today—with the promise of help from Gov. Henry F. Schricker.

He said he went to Indianapolis the other day to buy a net for friend turtle—affectionately dubbed "Oscar"—but failed in his shopping trip.

However, Harris said, he did run into the governor who chatted with him for a while about elusive Oscar. Harris quoted Schricker as saying:

"If you need any help, feel free to call on me."

Harris has had plenty of "help" since the turtle hunting started. He found more of the same when he returned to Churubusco—this time from Robert Webber, Indianapolis businessman.

Webber suggested that Harris let him freeze the lake in easy stages, section by section. Harris said the idea would be to freeze Oscar "loose" from the murky depths and send him scooting for shore and warmer climes.

The farmer, hounded by thousands of visitors since the turtle affair started last spring when the lake was frozen over, said he thinks it will be easier to drain the lake. And anyway, he said, he's already doing it.

Turtle Hunter Resumes Hunt

CHURUBUSCO, INDIANA—Crowd gathered on shore to watch Gale Harris and his aides (in boat at right) as they attempt in vain to capture Oscar the giant turtle, which Harris claims is at the bottom of the lake, on his farm near here. Most of the lake has already been pumped out in quest of the turtle.

New Castle News, October 25, 1949, page 5.

The Galveston Daily News reported on November 14, 1949:

Farmer Falls Victim to Own Trap

CHUHUBUSCO, Ind. Nov. 13.
(UP)—Farmer Gale Harris, angered by falling a victim of his own trap, said today he was ready to make his "biggest try yet" at capturing the monster turtle of Fulk's Lake.

Harris revealed that he had a narrow escape last week when he fell into a deep crevice formed in the lake bottom of the draining operations he has carried out for weeks in an effort to expose the turtle.

REDUCES LAKE
He now has the lake reduced to a quarter acre in size and is equipped with a net twice that big which he plans to drag across the area.

"It's a grudge fight to the finish now," he said.

Harris said he sank into the crevice up to his waist and had to be rescued by a human chain formed by neighbors.

That's what made him more determined than ever to snare the turtle, which has eluded his every effort since last spring.

The farmer, and some others in the area, believing that the turtle is 500 years old and weighs at least 500 pounds.

REPORT JEALOUSY
Harris dismissed as "pure jealousy" the report of Woodrow Rigsby at Fort Wayne that he had captured a 100-pound turtle in another lake five miles away. Rigsby did not claim that his turtle was Harris' turtle.

Harris said Rigsby worked with him earlier in trying to capture the Fulk's Lake monster and was trying to make him jealous.

"That other turtle is no 100 pounds, either," Harris said. "I looked at it and it's no more than 70, if that much. Besides, he imported it from Missouri."

After this, the media flurry around Oscar slowly died out, while some doubted the titanic turtle was ever there to begin with. However, it should also be noted that 200 people gathered at the lake claimed to have seen Oscar's head break the surface in an effort to catch a duck on the water. That's pretty good evidence for the creature's existence.

It's also important to note, though, that only a year later in Black Oak, Indiana, a Lake County Surveyor and a farmer drained a swamp and did find a huge turtle with a head as "big as a human's."[28] Did Oscar move, or was that just another oversized cousin?

While those with a skeptical attitude will doubt the existence of Oscar in favor of his presence being a tourism scam on the part of Harris, one must remember the considerable effort Harris put into finding Oscar. Furthermore, it is doubtful the crowds gathered around the lake were enough to pay for the earlier shenanigans, not to mention Harris's crops crushed at the feet of thousands of onlookers. It truly seems Harris was a man determined to prove what he saw was real, not to make dishonest dollars. And again, Harris gained nothing from the affair. In fact, he seemed to lose a great deal.

---

[28] Coleman and Huyghe, *Field Guide to Lake Monsters, Sea Serpents, and Other Mystery Denizens of the Deep*, pp.175-176.

'Turtle Day'

Churubusco Puts 'Oscar' To Work For Good of Town

CHURUBUSCO, Ind., July 27 — (UP)—Churubusco switched its giant turtle hunt that once turned a farmer's dreams of riches into rags into a fund-raising campaign to pay off the mortgage on a community building today.

Farmer Gale Harris went broke last year after months of delving into the murky depths of Fulks lake in search of "Oscar," a giant turtle Harris said was as big as a dining room table.

The town—plagued with a $5,000 mortgage on a boy scout and community building—was quick to latch onto the possibilities of the thousands who followed the turtle hunt. Churches, fraternal groups and businessmen banded together to stage a "Turtle Day" in an attempt to pay off the mortgage. The mortgage was cut in half, and the town decided to make it an annual affair.

Although no one has searched for the turtle since Harris sold his farm and left the community, the town still believes in Oscar.

"The natives are pretty sure Oscar exists," said Pat Isay, an insur-

ance man and one of the workers who planned Turtle Day.

"We're convinced Oscar is out there. Too many people have seen him for it to be a hoax," Isay said.

Turtle Day,—featuring everything from a piecating contest to the crowning of a queen by Rep. E. Ross Adair—was launched with a mechanical turtle fashioned from a big truck.

A thunderstorm broke shortly before the big turtle rolled through the streets. But Isay said it would take "more than that to dampen our spirits."

"This thing has created a brotherly spirit around town," Isay said. "It's the first time all groups have worked on one common cause and it seems to last all year 'round."

The community building was built on two acres of ground just outside of Churubusco. When the town gets the building paid for it plans another campaign to raise money to improve the grounds.

But the man who started it all wasn't expected to be around. Isay said no one had been able to contact Harris or his turtle.

Valparaiso Vidette Messenger (July 27, 1951).

Churubusco wasted no time in promoting the incident, though, and the first Turtle Days Festival was held in 1950 in hopes of raising funds to alleviate a $5,000 mortgage on a boy scout and community building. Now, 59 years later, Churubusco's Turtle Days Festival, held every year in mid-June, is the longest-running festival in Indiana. During the celebration nearly 2,000 tourists show up to enjoy the festivities, which include rides, entertainment, parades, vendors with turtle memorabilia, turtle-inspired dishes, and, most importantly, watch the four-hour-long turtle race.

Sources:

Cohen, Daniel. *The Encyclopedia of Monsters.* Dodd, Mead, 1982.

Coleman, Loren and Patrick Huyghe. *The Field Guide to Lake Monsters, Sea Serpents, and Other Mystery Denizens of the Deep.* Penguin, 2003.

LeMay, John. *Roswell USA: Towns That Celebrates UFOs, Bigfoot, and Other Weirdness.* Roswell Books, 2011.

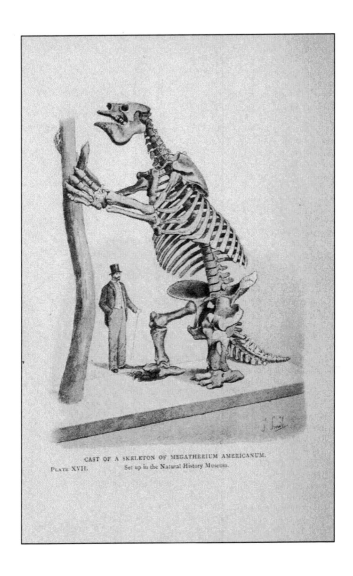

CAST OF A SKELETON OF MEGATHERIUM AMERICANUM.

PLATE XVII.   Set up in the Natural History Museum.

GIANT SLOTHS OF
THE AMERICAS
Beasts of Boonville and Sherman

DOWN IN SOUTH AMERICA there was a rash of giant sloth sightings throughout the late 1800s and early 1900s. Collectively known as the Neomylodon, there were two varieties, the larger Megatherium and the slightly smaller Mylodon. And though they may not sound intimidating, to those that allegedly saw them in South America, they were both vicious and terrifying.

Though North America was also home to giant ground sloths in the Pleistocene, modern day sightings of them were rare compared to South America. However, there are still a few. What may have been a giant sloth terrorized residents of Boonville, Indiana, in the summer of 1937.

Initially, the beast was thought to be an ape, though later the theory was put forth that it was a giant sloth. Below is one of the only articles I could find on the sightings from the *Tipton Daily Tribune* of August 16, 1937:

STRANGE BEAST NEAR BOONVILLE

Children Are Kept Home at Night and Hunters Scour Woods.

MAY BE GREAT APE

Boonville, Aug. 15. — A giant beast which lets out blood-curdling screams in the middle of the night and leaves footprints which are larger than a human's is terrifying residents along the Ohio River near Cypress beach, a few miles south of here.

Mothers are keeping their children indoors as searching parties scour nearby woods.

The strange animal first was heard a year ago near the home of Ralph Duff, a fisherman living near the river. Duff's police dog had to be killed after it came away from a battle with its fur in shreds and its jawbones crushed.

Friday night the Duffs heard the same beastly howl. Mrs. Duff saw a towering monster, as large as a huge bear. She screamed and the beast ran away.

Fearful of an early return, Duff has set a number of bear traps. Several residents believe that the animal is a huge ape which may live in a cave along the river.

188

SOUNDS LIKE A BEAR YARN

BOONVILLE, Ind., Aug. 16. — (INS). — They're looking for a hairy ape near here today after a monster has terrorized this community.

Persons living near Cypress beach, a few miles south of here, have told tales of encountering a giant beast which specializes in blood-curdling screams in the middle of the night and leaves footprints larger than a human's.

Ralph Duff, a fisherman, first reported the animal about a year ago after his police dog was torn to shreds in an encounter with the beast.

This week-end Mrs. Duff said she heard a terrifying howl late In the night and saw a tower monster larger than a bear. When she screamed, the beast ran away.

Duff believes that the animal is a huge ape, which lives in one of the caves along the river, and has set a number of bear traps.

A variant of the same article from the *Hammond Times* (August 16, 1937).

Believe Boonville Monster is Harmless Giant Sloth

BOONVILLE, Ind., Aug. 19 — (UP)—A stranger who declined to identify himself strolled into the newspaper office here today and declared that the weird, mysterious beast whose screams and prowlings have terrified residents of the Ohio river valley is simply a giant sloth.

The man said he and his uncle were returning from Mexico two years ago with the sloth, which they had captured on a game hunting expedition. He said they lost it near Evansville and never had found a trace of it since. He was uncertain if it was two-toed or three-toed, but averred that sloths came in both varieties.

When a sloth is hungry and frightened, he said, it will give vent to blood-curdling shrieks and yells such as terrified river valley residents have reported they have heard intermittently since Friday night.

At that time Mrs. Ralph Duff reported she caught a fleeting glimpse of the animal and said it looked like an ape.

Posses, according to reports here, are searching the river bottoms cautiously in the hope of tracking the beast to its lair.

River folk said today that they had seen an empty circus truck in the vicinity, and assumed that animal experts are endeavoring to capture the alleged monster also.

Read the Classified Ads

Logansport Pharos Tribune (August 19, 1937).

Other reports I've found indicate that traps with raw meat were also laid but nothing was ever caught, and by August 19th, some papers declared that the search was being "temporarily abandoned." I found another interesting report from the *Logansport Pharos Tribune* of August 19, 1937, which related that an anonymous stranger told the paper that the creature was possibly a large ground sloth which he brought with him from Mexico! He claimed that it had escaped from him two years ago in the area. Perhaps he captured a younger variety of Mylodon which matured over the next two years until it became the Boonville Monster? After all, it did apparently maul a dog to death and people thought it big enough to be either a bear or a gorilla. Whatever the case, the creature wasn't seen again, and the sighting is sometimes mistakenly conglomerated with the Thorntown gorilla hoax of 1949,[29] which has led some to completely dismiss this case.

Vintage Depiction of Giant Ground Sloth.

Moving on from Indiana, our next giant sloth sightings come from New York State of all places. We'll begin with this article from *The Evening World* of April 30, 1905:

---

[29] A simple affair of hoaxers trampling through the woods in a bear suit mistaken for a gorilla.

QUEER LOOKING MONSTER DUG OUT OF ROCKS.

Long, Hairy Animal Scared Workmen After a Blast on West Side.

Whether it was a jabberwock, a Bandersnatch, a jub-jub bird or a snark that emerged from the bowels of the earth in this city to-day, causing thirty workmen to drop their tools of trade and take to the highest points in sight is a moted question. That it was something fully as bad as any beast in the late Mr. Carroll's menagerie, there can be no doubt. Zoologists are cordially invited to the saloon at Sixty-fourth street and Amsterdam avenue to view it and pass an opinion on genus and habitat.

What happened was this: Thirty workmen, honest Irish sons of toil, with an Italian scattered here and there among them, were busily engaged today in making deeper the hole on Sixty-third street near Eleventh avenue, where the foundation for the first of Henry Philipps's model tenements is to be laid, when out from between the ruins of a giant rock which had just crumbled from blasting powder, came a queer hairy animal, as long as a man, with legs like those of an orangutan and a head the size of an orange.

A creature so ridiculously out of proportion according to modern standards could only be of some prehistoric monster, and however interesting such may be to naturalists, they are not the least bit so to the knights of the pick and the spade.

The little cluster of whiskers in the centre of old Terence McManus's throat stood out at a fearful angle when his eyes lighted on the creature.

Then down went Terry's pick into the earth and up when his voice to the heavens in a shriek that fair froze the blood in the veins of his comrades.

"Howly mither! Luk at it, luk at it!" wailed Terry, and, of course, everybody took a look.

Then there was quick action, and in less than thirty seconds the monster had the hole to itself. Along the edges, scared, white faces peered over at it. They saw a long, sinuous body and muscular legs, with three fierce talons at the end of each foot. They saw a foolish little head in the centre of it, two beady black eyes. They saw a tail that curled at the end and a body full of irregular bumps.

Leisurely around the hole went the monster. Then it decided to climb out. There was a scattering of citizens at once. Big Pat Coughlin didn't get out of the way in time, and before he knew it the monster was close to him. Pat didn't wait to learn whether or not its intentions were hostile. He just swung the spade which he had clung to around at it and landed on the top of its little head. There was a crack and the monster rolled over for the count. Before he could get up again some of the others landed on him with rocks and he gave up the ghost.

Then he was carried into the saloon where Big Pat sold him as a curiosity, the gang taking the price out in mixed ale. The only animal expert around Eleventh avenue gave it as his opinion, that the beast was a South American sloth.

"I was down there once," he said, "and seen them hanging to trees by them talons. It's a sloth, that's what it is."

No one could explain how a South American sloth could get from his habitat on the Amazon river to an Eleventh avenue excavation, but there he was, and he is on view for the skeptical.

I wouldn't have bothered with the odd account above if not for a far more interesting account from New York sixty years later. Afterall, the creature killed in 1905 sounded to be a normal, albeit out-of-place ground sloth rather than a Mylodon. However, if a report from the mid-1960s is true, then the little creature may have been a baby Mylodon rather than a full-grown sloth.

After attaining a reputation for mysterious creatures since his famous Mothman investigation in the 1960s, John Keel soon began receiving letters telling of other monsters. In 1970, he received one from a young man from Sherman, New York. He claimed that about five years ago he had witnessed two large hairy creatures he couldn't identify:

I am writing because about three or four years ago, [circa. 1965-66] I saw a white monster in a swamp beside our house. I have been seeing these things ever since then and close to our house. One night it came down in our yard. It stands between twelve and eighteen feet high, it has a long tail between six and eight feet long. It is all covered with hair. They are always white. I have seen them alone or two at a time. It can walk on two feet or four feet. It is almost a double for a Prehistoric Sloth. My whole family has seen this thing and I know of two more men who have seen them... I am fifteen years old and I am not kidding. I have seen these things and they are real."[30]

Say of it what you will, but Keel thought enough of the account to publish it in his *The Complete Guide to Mysterious Beings*. Though there's certainly not a dearth of sightings when compared to creatures like Bigfoot, it would seem there is a possibility that giant sloths recently roamed North America.

Sources:

Keel, John. *The Complete Guide to Mysterious Beings*. (2014 reprint)

---

[30] Keel, *Complete Guide to Mysterious Beings*, Kindle Edition, p.121.

The Iceman

Minnesota Iceman as it appeared in the
Des Moines Register on August 24, 1969.

THE MINNESOTA ICEMAN
Cave Man Hoax or the Real Article?

IN THE LATE 1960s, a lucky few were able to observe the frozen body of a "man left over from the Ice Age" at various fairs and events throughout the U.S.[31] The block of ice containing the body was kept in a refrigerated glass coffin of sorts and was exhibited by Frank D. Hansen. Though today known as the Minnesota Ice Man, for its first few years on exhibition it was called the 'Siberskoye Creature'. And, it may well have retained that name and faded into obscurity if not for having been seen by Terry Cullen at the International Livestock Exposition's annual fair in Chicago in

---

[31] Contrary to some reports, it was never a "carnival attraction".

1968. Cullen was a zoology major who just happened to know naturalist Ivan T. Sanderson... who just happened to have Bernard Heuvelmans as a houseguest at the time. As such, the two greatest cryptozoologists of their time were on hand to examine the body.

Hansen allowed the two naturalists into his small Minnesota-based trailer in December of 1968 to examine the frozen cadaver. Beneath the ice they observed a muscular, man-like corpse lying on its back, the left arm distinctively twisted behind its head with the right arm on the torso. The hands were quite large, and the broad face was neanderthal-like, with a short, upturned nose and a prominent brow. Through the ice they were also able to observe various wounds on the body along with its genitalia. The duo was even able to smell a slight purification of the flesh from out of some of the melted ice when it accidentally cracked during the investigation. As such, and after three days' worth of examinations, Sanderson and Heuvelmans were convinced of the corpse's authenticity.

Despite Hansen's wishes, Sanderson and Heuvelmans went public on the matter in 1969. Heuvelmans excitedly described the body in *The Bulletin of the Royal Institute of Natural Sciences of Belgium* as resembling a six-foot-tall man, only "excessively hairy." Heuvelmans went on that "It is entirely covered with very dark brown hair three to four inches long. Its skin appears waxlike, similar in color to the cadavers of white men not tanned by the sun."

Sanderson described the body in the May 1969 issue of *Argosy*, pointing out its grotesque eyes which had popped out of the skull. One was missing, and the other was barely visible under the ice, and blood was discernable as it oozed from the sockets.

May 1969 issue of *Argosy*.

Sanderson even mentioned the creature on *The Tonight Show with Johnny Carson* during the

Christmas week of 1968. And while Heuvelmans gave it the scientific name of *Homo pongoides* ('ape-like man'), Sanderson took to calling it Bozo. However, neither name stuck, and it was called the Minnesota Ice Man.

Frank Hansen with the Minnesota Iceman, though it's unknown if this was the original or the duplicate.

However, as with any major cryptozoological discovery, there were some problems with the pedigree of the find. One of the issues with the body was Hansen's varying stories as to how it was procured. Initially, he claimed that the body was found incased in a block of ice as it floated across the Siberian coast by a Russian seal-hunting vessel. Then it switched to a Japanese whaling ship. Next up came the rumor it was discovered in deepfreeze in a Hong Kong facility.

A more American explanation surfaced when a woman named Helen Westring came forth and claimed she had shot it in the eye while hunting in the Whiteface Reservoir region of Minnesota in 1966.

Westring's Story Cont'd

According to "On the Trail of Monsters" by Nicholas Von Hoffman in *The Brainerd Daily Dispatch* of August 19, 1976:

Helen Westring, who several years ago claimed to have been raped by an Abominable Snowman in Bemidji, Minnesota, of all places. Her story which appeared as a first-person account in a periodical called "The National Bulletin," made Fay Wray's prehistoric lover, Kong, appear the soul of consideration.

Ms. Westring took her trusty rifle and shot her assailant, who was later identified as the Minnesota Iceman, a local monster of the upper Midwest whose short lifespan was a result not of the bullet but of the conviction the poor fellow was a carnival hoax.

Still, the most accepted theory as to the body's origin was that it was an ape-man killed in Vietnam and flown to the States. This also tracked with a story that Heuvelmans had heard of an ape-like creature killed in Danang, Vietnam, in 1966. Not coincidentally, this was also where Hansen was said to have been stationed during the war. However, Hansen always claimed that it was not he who owned the body. He stated multiple times that it belonged to a secret, wealthy owner in California and that he was just the temporary ward.[32]

Problems arose with the Minnesota Ice Man story when John Napier, a primatologist at the Smithsonian Institute, was invited to examine the body. To Napier, it looked like a fake. Hansen then explained that it was in this case, stating that he had returned the real specimen to its anonymous wealthy owner. And why had he done this? That's because, like Helen Westring's probably made-up story, there was a possibility that Hansen himself shot the man-like being when it was alive and feared criminal charges. As such, some think that Hansen hid the real body for that reason.

'Creature' Stirs Doubt, Belief at Great Lakes Mall Exhibit

The Willoughby News Herald (headline above) of July 19, 1973, reported that,

Later the creature's anonymous owner denied the Smithsonian permission to examine

---

[32] Though the name was never disclosed, for some reason it's believed that it may have been actor Jimmy Stewart of all people.

it. The institution, FBI and U.S. Department of Health, Education and Welfare tried seizing it at customs in Portal, N.D.

Sen. Walter Mondale (D-Minn) stopped the seizure.

Sanderson backed up the claim of a duplicate body replacing the real one, stating that the new "cadaver" was different from the one he had examined previously. This can also be seen in photos of the Minnesota Iceman, which show differences in the face and the poses of the body. For instance, in some photographs the mouth is closed while in others it's open. Among those who photographed the decoy body was Loren Coleman, who saw it on exhibit in 1969 and showed his photos to Sanderson, who confirmed it was a different body. Regardless of this, ever since, the Minnesota Ice Man has been labeled as a hoax.

Shades Of The Piltdown Man And Cardiff Giant

Ice Man May Be Another Hoax

Headline in the *Defiance Crescent News* of April 11, 1969.

However, even if the second body was a replica, one cannot discount the fact that Sanderson and Heuvelmans both smelt rotting flesh during their 1968 examination. Some also have suggested that the putrefaction smell was a carnival trick as well, but Coleman reported he noted no smell when he observed the Iceman in 1969. And, again, the smell didn't arise until Heuvelmans accidentally cracked the glass with a hot lamp. Under the circumstances, one could consider it a lucky accident. Considering the smell and also the changing appearance of the body, it makes more sense that the real article was simply returned to its mystery owner and replaced with a double as opposed to having been a hoax all along.

Sources:

Coleman, Loren. *Mysterious America* (Revised Edition). Paraview Press, 2001.

Coleman, Loren & Jerome Clark. *Cryptozoology A to Z.* Fireside, Simon & Schuster Ltd, 1999.

Heuvelmans, Bernard. "Note preliminaire sur un specimen conserve dans la glace, d'une forme encore inconnue d'hominide vivant Homo pongoides." *Bulletin de I'Institut Royal des Science Naturelles de Belgique* 45 (1969).

Naish, Darren. "The Strange Case of the Minnesota Iceman." Scientific American. (January 2, 2017) https://blogs.scientificamerican.com/tetrapod-zoology/the-strange-case-of-the-minnesota-iceman/#

JUNKYARD LIZARD
The Milton Monster

YOU'VE HEARD OF junkyard dogs, but what about a junkyard lizard? In the summer of 1975, reports were made in Trimble County, Kentucky, of a gigantic reptile roaming the land. Specifically, it resembled a much larger than normal monitor lizard—about fifteen feet long—and was sighted in the vicinity of Canip Creek, adjacent to the Ohio River northeast of Milton, Kentucky.

The story began on July 3, 1975, when the *Trimble County Banner* published a photo of strange animal tracks going through the tomato field of Carl Abbot. The four-toed prints were clawed and measured four and a half by five inches. In addition to the tracks, the previous evening Abbot had heard menacing noises coming from an unseen animal. Furthermore, a neighbor's dog had recently been attacked by an unknown predator which left deep gashes in its side.

This was simply the prelude to the more notable sightings to take place in the Blue Grass Body Shop, a junk and wrecking yard operated by two brothers, Clarence "Toughy" Cable and Garrett Cable. On July 26th, Clarence was walking through the junkyard when from behind some debris near a wrecked van emerged a huge lizard.[33] He would later describe it as looking similar to a monitor lizard, though not exactly identical to one. He didn't give exact measurements in that case other than to say it was about the size of a man with legs eight-to-ten inches long. It hissed at him several

---

[33] Some sources place this sighting as happening three weeks earlier.

times, and he described it as having "big eyes similar to a frog's." It also had a long, forked tongue—long meaning nearly one foot in this case. He described the skin as being off-white on the underbelly below the mouth. As for the rest of the body color, he said it had "black and white stripes cross ways of its body with quarter-sized speckles over it."[34]

Garrett Cable was the next to see the monster. On July 27th while working in the junkyard, he noticed a pile of old car hoods beginning to shake and vibrate. Soon, the head and shoulders of a huge lizard emerged from under the pile of hoods. Garrett ran to get Clarence, but when the brothers returned to the pile of hoods, they couldn't find the animal anywhere.

On the 28th, another even bigger lizard was seen by Clarence. Though no measurement was given of the first two sightings, this time Cable estimated the creature's length to be 15 feet. Cable threw a rock at the monster, which hissed at him and then rushed into the brush to hide. Cable went inside his home to get a rifle, which he used to shoot into the brush in hopes of hitting the monster. A search party began scouring the area in the first days of August surrounding the wrecking yard but found nothing dead or alive.

Eventually the moniker of the Milton Lizard was bestowed upon the cryptid, although it was also sometimes called the Canip Monster. The story

---

[34] Another source specifically described them as orange specks across its head and back.

was popular in the *Trimble Banner*, which interviewed Clarence Cable several times. Cable's best guess as to how the monster got there was that one of the wrecked vehicles they had acquired must have had the creature's egg in it and it hatched in the junkyard where it grew up. Cable theorized that perhaps the car came from one of the warmer western states. Cable further theorized that they had seen the beast only recently because they had cleared out some excess wreckage the previous spring, thus giving the lizard fewer places to hide. However, Cable and the press were unaware of several other nearby lizard sightings from years before. Not too far away from Milton is Crosswicks, Ohio, where a similar lizard monster was seen. Actually, more than seen, this creature mauled a young boy. Furthermore, this creature was bipedal like a theropod dinosaur.

The encounter took place in May of 1882. An article on it detailed a monster quite similar to the Milton Lizard, with "legs four feet long". It reported:

Feet about twelve inches long and shaped like a lizard's, of black and white color, with large yellow spots. Head about sixteen inches wide, with a long, black forked tongue and the mouth inside deep red. The hind legs appeared to be used to give it an erect position, and its propelling power is in its tail.

Another similar creature was seen around Zanesville, Ohio, in the 1880s as well.

The Crosswicks Monster.
(Courtesy Warren County Historical Society).

Luckily for us, seasoned cryptozoologist Mark A. Hall investigated the Canid Monster case himself four years later in 1979. What he uncovered linked the monster to the Crosswicks creature in more ways than general location. For starters, the two cryptids had similar coloring. Also like the Crosswicks monster, Hall found a few witnesses who said that Milton Lizard was occasionally seen in a bipedal stance like a theropod.[35]

---

[35] Perhaps this is neither here nor there, but Trimble County also has legends of Frogmen. The Milton Lizard's eyes were described as frog-like, which is interesting, and as just reported, it was sometimes said to be bipedal.

In light of Hall's findings, could it be possible that the "Milton Lizard" was also a theropod dinosaur similar to the Crosswicks Monster as opposed to an overgrown Monitor Lizard? Considering it was never seen again after 1975, we will never know.

Sources:

Hall, Mark A. *Natural Mysteries: Monster Lizards, English Dragons, and Other Puzzling Animals* (2nd ed.) Mark A. Hall Publications and Research, 1991.

SIDE STORY
ANOTHER BIG LIZARD

The *Logansport Pharos Tribune* of November 3, 1910, reported:

SHOOTS A STRANGE REPTILE

Richmond Hunter Brings Down Curiosity and presents it to Earlham

Richmond, Ind. Nov. 3.—The creature resembles several kinds of reptiles. It has a tail about one and one-half feet long and similar to that of a snake. It has four legs, resembling those of an alligator, except the toes, the ends of which are hooked like claws. Its body is like that of a lizard, only much larger than those seen in that section and covered with a tough skin. On its back is a furlike ridge. The head is very large, resembling a fish, while under the head and attached to the throat is a large pouch. The animal measures five feet in length and weighs about eighteen pounds. It has been presented to the Earlham College Museum.

Recent depiction of the Snallygaster from
Lumberwoods, Unnatural History Museum.
(http://www.lumberwoods.org/)

THE SNALLYGASTER
The Bootleggers and the Beast

ONE OF THE MORE famous monsters of the early 20th Century was undoubtedly the Snallygaster of Maryland. Tales of the creature came with German immigrants who settled in Frederick County in the 1730s. Folk tales abound of something called the Schneller Geist ("quick ghost" in German) terrorizing the area. A precursor to the Snallygaster that would emerge hundreds of years later, the Schneller Geist was basically a gigantic demon bird. Tales of the monster died out as times changed but were resurrected to frighten freed slaves in the post-Civil War landscape.

For whatever reason, in 1909, the Schneller Geist returned as the Snallygaster. Descriptions of the cryptid were truly wild. Though essentially just a giant bird, it possessed only a single eye in the middle of its forehead and tentacles like an octopus either trailing behind it near the tail or extending from the mouth in some illustrations.[36]

This article, sans a headline, was retrieved from the *Shepherdstown Register* of February 4, 1909, and compared the Snallygaster to the Jersey Devil. The article also illustrated how the Snallygaster was used to intimidate the African American population:

We look for a considerable scare among the colored people of this section, for the terrible beast that has been causing so much alarm in New Jersey is undoubtedly headed this way. The creature was first heard from in New Jersey about a month ago, when its tracks in the snow were observed. They could be seen in a field, and then they would suddenly disappear. This was the source of much mystery until it was discovered that the fearful beast could fly as well as it could walk. James Harding was the first man to see it, and he described it as a sort of cross between a vampire, a tiger and a bovalipus. It has enormous wings, a long, pointed bill, four legs armed with claws like steel hooks, one eye in the center of its forehead, and screeches like a locomotive whistle. A colored man by the name of Bill Gifferson was a victim of the go-devil, or

---

[36] I would be remiss in not noting that the Crawfordsville Monster was also reported to have feathers and a singular eye.

whatever it may be called. He was walking along a country road, when it swooped down upon him, carried him to the top of a high hill, and, piercing his jugular vein with its needle-like bill, slowly sucked his blood while it gently fanned him with its wings.

The beast was seen near Hagerstown last week. George Jacobs was out hunting, when he saw a strange looking thing flying over his head. He thoughtlessly fired at it, but the shot rattled from its tough hide as if he had shot against an iron plate. The enraged go-devil whirled around after him and he barely escaped by dodging into a stable and slamming the door. Its yawps were fearful. It is said that it laid an egg near Half Way—an egg almost as large as a barrel, covered with a tough, parchment-like shell of a yellowish color.

What alarms us is that the awful creature is reported to have been seen near Sharpsburg and that it is believed to have taken up its abode in the cave along the cliffs known as "Tobey's hole," about a half mile above Shepherdstown.

This vampire-devil only attacks colored people. It is a native of Senegambia, where only colored people live, and so it has never acquired a taste for white persons. It is seldom seen during the day, feeding at night only, and the strange part is that it seems to prefer colored men to colored women, though it attacks the latter at times. It never gets after children, unless very hungry, as they do not have sufficient blood to satisfy it.

The latest report is that the government intends to send a troop of United States soldiers and a Gatling gun to Shepherdstown with the hope that they can kill the dreadful monster. The Smithsonian Institute, however, wishes to capture it alive.

Latest—The monster was seen last night by a Norfolk & Western engineer, near Antietam Station. It was flying about fifty feet from the ground, and it appeared to him to be about the size of a large horse.

Though I had read reports before that the Snallygaster caught the attention of the Smithsonian and then President Theodore Roosevelt, I tend to think that's hearsay. The article seems to exist more than anything to demean the African American population, and the newspapers often claimed that the Smithsonian was coming to investigate this or that when the Smithsonian never had any such plans. And while Roosevelt certainly had an interest in mystery animals,[37] I find it doubtful he would be gullible enough to believe the article just printed, or any variation of it.

While the article just discussed may be purely satiric, the papers did receive letters from people who may have actually sighted a strange, flying creature. One of the letters came from a man in

---

[37] Roosevelt heard tales of Bigfoot, and later in life would embark on an expedition in South America in hopes of spotting a remnant plesiosaurus.

Casstown, Ohio, who told the *Valley Register* that he had seen the monster fly over his area. It made terrible screeching noises, and its description could fit a pterodactyl quite well, as he said it had two huge wings, a 20-foot tail, and a "horny head." While this report at first seems encouraging, it was actually written by Thomas C. Harbaugh, a friend of *Middletown Valley Register* editor George C. Rhoderick. And the credibility gets worse from there.

It was next sighted in Maryland by a man who operated a brick-burning kiln near Cumberland. The man found it near his kiln, fast asleep when it awoke. It let out its signature screech and then flew away. Or, that's what some cryptozoological posts simply report in an effort to cover up just how ludicrous the sighting actually was. In reality, the newspaper article claimed that the creature spoke, saying, "My, I'm dry! I haven't had a good drink since I was killed in the Battle of Chickamauga!" (This odd statement would seem to make the implication that the monster either took part in the famous Civil War battle or was a ghostly spirit resulting from a death in the battle.)

Next it was seen flying over the mountains between Gapland and Burkittsville as well as the Hagerstown vicinity. At one of these places it laid yet another egg. At least one report claimed that a man had taken in the egg to incubate it. A Snallygaster hunt ensued, and at least one casualty occurred in the form of a large owl that was for a time displayed as the legendary beast.

The last of the 1909 flap occurred at an Emmitsburg, Frederick County, train station in March. There the monster swooped down from the skies to grab Ed Brown by the suspenders. Another man was on hand to grab onto Brown's foot, and his suspender snapped in the struggle, bringing him back to the ground. The Snallygaster continued to torment the men and a fight erupted. No less than three men tangled with the monster, which began shooting fire from its nostrils. Not even gunfire could drive it away. Eventually an Emmitsburg deputy, Norman Hoke, came onto the scene, pulled out his badge, and ordered the monster away. At that, the Snallygaster retreated into the woods. Though Norman Hoke was a real man, the story obviously was not.

For 23 years, the newspapers let the creature sleep. But reports of the monster had left its mark on superstitious farmers, who painted seven-pointed stars on their barns in hopes of warding off the beast. Then, in 1932, it returned with a vengeance. Therefore, some presumed that the "new" Snallygaster was the result of one of the eggs laid in 1909.

Again reports flooded newspapers and the Snallygaster tale even made it onto national radio via a report from Lowell Thomas. By December, the monster's reign of terror was over. The December 21ˢᵗ edition of the *Hagerstown Morning Herald* screamed, "Death of Snallygaster Is Reported: Accounts Differ." The monster met its end while flying over Frog Hollow, a notorious moonshine still in Washington County. As it circled an illegal distillery, the fumes from a 2,5000 gallon vat of liquor proved to be too much for the creature, which was "overcome and fell directly into the mash." Workers ran out of the still in a panic, and the scene was soon investigated by officers George T. Danforth and Charles E. Cushwa, with the former offering the statement, "Imagine our feeling when our eyes feasted on the monster submerged in the liquor vat."

Like the deputy from the March 1909 article, these two men were also real. Susan Fair surmised in her wonderful *Mysteries and Lore of Western Maryland: Snallygasters, Dogmen and Other Mountain Tales*:

> George Danforth was an actual agent in Hagerstown at this time, and Charles Cushwa was a sheriff's deputy. The connection of these two very real gentlemen to this story implies that one of two unlikely things must be true: either there really was a Snallygaster found drowned in a vat of moonshine in Washington County in 1932 or Prohibition agents had a really good sense of humor. I'll leave it up to the reader to determine which is more likely.[38]

Furthermore, it was said that nothing but the monster's skeleton remained after having been eaten away by a large amount of lye in the moonshine. The Prohibition agents then blew up both the still and the monster's remains with 500

---

[38] Fair, *Mysteries and Lore of Western Maryland*, pp.19-20.

pounds of dynamite. Therefore, the monster's body couldn't be examined by experts.

Scene and Incident of Snallygaster's Reign

Some have since speculated that Prohibition-era moonshiners began making up new tales of the Snallygaster to explain noises coming from their distilleries, such as explosions and the clanging of metal work. It's possible that reports of noises came first and sightings of the monster shortly after—those being supplied by the bootleggers.

Or, if not that, the *Middletown Valley Register* simply decided to cook up another Snallygaster scare for whatever reason. Whatever the case, other papers jumped on the bandwagon and supposedly *National Geographic* was making plans to get a photo of the monster. Was *National Geographic* really that gullible? Who knows, but it's probably not a coincidence that the monster's death was reported shortly thereafter.

Could there have been any truth at all to the sightings? Did at least one witness, perhaps, sight a real cryptid, even if all the other reports were pure fiction? Probably not. Most likely the Maryland newspaper publishers took note of how the Jersey Devil increased paper sales in 1909 and decided to create their own monster, which they based off the old folk superstition of the Schneller Geist. Though a fun piece of folklore, ultimately the tale of the Snallygaster is likely only that.

Sources:

Fair, Susan. *Mysteries and Lore of Western Maryland: Snallygasters, Dogmen and Other Mountain Tales.* The History Press, 2013.

NOT A RATTLER: Dr. Ivo Poglayen, director of the Rio Grande Zoo, examines the skin of a giant snake on exhibit at Ruidoso. Dr. Poglayen said the skin did not come from a rattlesnake as two Ruidoso men who turned up with the skin insist. Instead, Dr. Poglayen said, the skin came from a member of the Boa Constrictor and Python snake family. The Journal flew Dr. Poglayen to Ruidoso for the examination Wednesday afternoon. (Journal photo)

Dr. Ivo Poglayen examines a large snakeskin
believed to have come from a giant rattlesnake.

GIANT SNAKES OF NEW MEXICO
Real and Imagined

IN WHAT WAS SURELY the strangest news to hit Southeastern New Mexico since the Roswell UFO Crash of 1947, the *Ruidoso News* reported that a giant rattlesnake had been killed near Carrizozo in July of 1960. The monster snake was shot by two Lincoln County men, 45-year-old Juan Baca and 46-year-old Mike Gonzales. The duo had taken their burros out to graze near the famous Valley of Fires lava beds when they spotted something peculiar in a dried-out pond bed: the ground seemed to be moving up and down.

Carrizozo's Valley of Fires.
(Historical Society for Southeast New Mexico)

Straight from the original July 12, 1960 *Roswell Daily Record* article "300-Pound Rattler: World's Largest?", here is the account:

"The ground seemed to be going up and down," [Gonzales] told [*Ruidoso News* Editor Vic Lamb]. It was the snake breathing.

Approaching to within 12 feet, he suddenly stopped, he said, frozen with fright. Gonzales had a Winchester with him and shot four times, missing every time as the snake raised its head five feet off the ground and "growled," rather than hissed.

"I was scared," Gonzales said.

Baca was some 200 feet away when he opened fire, aiming at the monster's backbone. All eight bullets hit the snake, but none of them penetrated the telephone-pole thickness of the frightful thing....Baca said smoke appeared to come out of the snake's body when the bullets struck home, but said it was probably dust.

The snake, in its death throws, stirred up a cloud of dust "like a herd of horses," Baca said.

Ruidoso News image from June 24, 1960.

The story caused a considerable stir across the state, with many other news services picking it up on the wire. One may now ask, just why did Vic Lamb and the rest of the press believe the fantastic story? As it turned out, the two ranchers had "proof" in the form of an 18-foot-long snakeskin which they brought with them into town ten days after shooting the reptile. The duo claimed they wanted to bring the snake back whole but couldn't figure out how to carry it. "It'd be too heavy for a horse," one of them said.

Within a few days, skeptical articles on the story naturally began to be printed, such as "Experts Don't Believe Snake is so Large" which reported:

Growing skepticism is being voiced about the 18 foot snake reportedly killed near Carrizozo.

SNAKE SLAYERS? — Although there is now a debate over whether the huge snake these men killed is a rattler or a bull snake, nevertheless, they experienced a terrifying several minutes in their encounter with the 18½ foot serpent in a dry lake bed north of the Malpais recently. Juan Baca, right, killed the snake with the gun he holds, while his companion, Mike Gonzales, shot the rifle he holds four times, missing every time from a distance of about 12 feet. Baca said he thought his lifetime friend was going to die of fright. "He turned white, then yellow, and looked awful sick." Baca said.

RUIDOSO NEWS PHOTO

Wayne Walker, El Paso curator, offered $100 an inch for any snake over eight feet long, with the view that his money is pretty safe.

Earlier this week Dr. Ivo Poglayen, director of the Rio Grande Park Zoo in Albuquerque, said such a snake as the one reported from Carrizozo would be a real "buzzer."

"About nine feet is the biggest one I ever heard of," Dr. Poglayen said. "I can barely believe 18 feet."

He said some snakes live to about 30 years in age and like all species of animal or reptile life have a maximum size. There is no species of snake in New Mexico that grows to an 18-foot length, he said. Such a size would be extremely large, even for a python.

Vic Lamb photo in *Ruidoso News.*

Another newspaper article reported that perhaps the snakeskin would go on display in the Smithsonian, and another claimed the two ranchers had been offered $750 for the skin. Ironically, this same skin eventually proved to be the story's downfall. Through the investigative prowess of Vic Lamb and his son, Jim Lamb, of the *Albuquerque Journal*, it was found that the snakeskin was actually that of a python. Jim Lamb tracked down an Albuquerque woman, Mrs. W.O. Edington, who claimed that the python skin had belonged to her, and she had previously thrown it away in a dumpster in Ruidoso, where she owned a cabin. The skin was then picked up by a trash man who traded it to Baca and Gonzales for ten chickens. The duo later said, "All we hoped to do was make a little money from selling the skin and we were misled by a third party into believing it was a genuine rattlesnake skin."[39]

Far more terrifying than the tale concocted by the hoaxers are stories of a giant rattlesnake living in the Guadalupe Mountains, which span lower Southeastern New Mexico and Western Texas. The giant snake is said to live in a mountain cave in association with a sinister tribe known as the Snake People.[40] Similar to the skinwalkers feared by the Navajo, the Snake People possess a powerful, dark medicine and many Native Americans are reluctant to speak of them. According to lore, these Snake People kept a giant rattlesnake in a cave in the Guadalupe Mountains that they offered sacrifices to. Supposedly these Snake People could even breed with rattlesnakes and turn themselves into snakes.

---

[39] "Apology is made about Snake Tale"
[40] Not to be confused with the Shoshone sometimes called the Snake Indians.

Two unidentified men with
large rattlesnakes in New Mexico.
(Historical Society for Southeast New Mexico)

The Mescalero Apache often talked of sheep
mysteriously disappearing in the area, while other
sheep found dead had so much rattlesnake venom
in their system that their insides were nearly
dissolved. One such Apache man in the 1940s was
working with two other sheepherders when a large
rattlesnake slithered into their camp. He told his
comrades it was a warning from the Snake People

to move their herd elsewhere. They only laughed at him and killed the snake. Two weeks later, they were dead by snakebite.

An Apache man called Mahlan told author Earl Murray a unique tale of the Snake People for his book *Ghosts of the Old West*. In 1982, Mahlan was going to visit his sister, who had married a rancher in Dog Canyon.[41] While exiting his vehicle to open the gate to his in-law's property, he claimed to see two huge, viper-like eyes illuminated in the darkness of night. From the illumination of the eyes, he could also make out a fork-like tongue darting from a huge mouth. He didn't just see the creature; he could also smell something that reminded him of a viper den. As if it were merely a vision, it eventually disappeared. When the man told his sister of the encounter, she admitted that she knew that the cave of the Snake People was nearby. To keep her family safe, she offered up their livestock to the Snake People on various occasions. She claimed that their grandfather had taken her to the opening of the evil cave when she was a girl and told her to be careful of the area. She saw no snakes, only a dark bottomless pit. When she tossed a rock into it, she heard what sounded like the buzzing of a thousand rattlesnakes, while an alternate account

---

[41] Actually, it's W.C. Jameson who cites the location as Dog Canyon in *Legend and Lore of the Guadalupe Mountains*. Murray never gives a place name. Furthermore, Jameson has this story taking place in the 1940s, so there's discrepancies between the two versions.

stated that the woman was forced to witness one of the sacrifices to the giant snake as well.

Mahlan's sister also told him that back in the 1940s, tales of the Snake People and their dark powers reached the government, which sent two anthropologists to investigate. The two men were lowered into the cave where the mysterious tribe supposedly still practiced via ropes operated by several ranchers and cowhands. The men above heard a great deal of screaming coming from below, as well as loud buzzing rattles, and tried to hoist the men back up. Only one of the men was pulled back out that day. He was dead and had an extremely high amount of rattlesnake venom in his system. One version of the story said his entire torso was in the process of being dissolved it had so much venom in it. The story concluded weeks later when the government sealed up the entrance to the cave with several tons of rock. Two weeks later a new entrance was clearly visible, with the appearance that something had pushed its way out from the cave.

Another big snake tale from the 1940s was told to authors Sherry Hansen-Steiger and Brad Steiger, which they published in their book *Montezuma's Serpent and Other Supernatural Tales of the Southwest*. A man identified as Reuben Montoya related that back in 1940 he lived in a New Mexico village with "much talk of witches and devils." He and his grandfather were walking through an arroyo at night when a gigantic rattlesnake materialized in front of them. It was as tall as a man when it reared up, and as big around as a large man's thigh. It came before Reuben and touched him with his tongue. Though young Reuben was unaware, the serpent was offering its tongue for him to kiss. Eventually the snake disappeared in a puff of smoke with a smell of "spent shotgun shells" and Reuben's grandfather began to weep. He told the boy that he had rejected an offer of wisdom and power from the spectral serpent. The angry grandfather slapped his grandson, and he ran home in tears. The following was presented to the Steigers not as a superstitious folktale, but as something that actually happened to the witness...

Sources:

Birchell, Donna Blake and John LeMay. *Hidden History of Southeast New Mexico*. The History Press, 2017.

Jameson, W.C. *Legend and Lore of the Guadalupe Mountains*. University of New Mexico Press, 2007.

Murray, Earl. *Ghosts of the Old West*. Dorset Press, 1988.

Steiger, Brad and Sherry Hansen-Steiger. *Montezuma's Serpent and Other Supernatural Tales of the Southwest*. Paragon House, 1992.

MINI MASTODONS OF WISCONSIN
Folklore At its Best

THIS IS ONE OF THOSE STORIES where it's tough to know just where to begin. We could start in the 1990s when it was first told to author Dennis Boyer in a Wisconsin bar. Or we could begin back in the 1930s, when most of the "action" took place. We could also start with what may be a quasi-related discovery from 1897 that probably influenced the story set in the 1930s.

We'll go about it chronologically for the sake of simplicity. In early July of 1897, the Boaz, Wisconsin, region had just endured a heavy rain, and as heavy rains do, they unearthed something interesting. On July 10, Harry, Chris, Verne, and Clyde Dosch (all brothers) stumbled across some gigantic bones as they surveyed the family farm for flood damage. The remains were found within Mill Creek and the brothers took it upon themselves to excavate them. Not knowing what the bones belonged to, they stood them up against their hitching post in the hopes that someone might identify them. That someone turned out to be the mailman, who spread the word until it reached the ears of Frank Burnham, attorney and member of the state legislature.

Boaz Mastodon on display at the UW-Madison Geology Museum c.1940s. (UW GEOLOGY MUSEUM)

Rather swiftly, Burnham bought the remains for a measly $50 and donated the bones, now recognized as belonging to a mastodon, to the state of Wisconsin. By 1915, they were being displayed in the University of Wisconsin museum as "The Boaz Mastodon."[42]

---

[42] In 2015, as the museum celebrated its 100th anniversary, an investigation showed that this was more of a "makeshift

Mammoth bones being excavated from Anderson Mills, which were later joined with the other remains to form the "Boaz Mastodon."
(UW GEOLOGY MUSEUM HISTORICAL COLLECTION)

Thanks to this celebrated discovery, Wisconsin was somewhat synonymous with mastodons for a time. As such, perhaps it's no surprise that a unique piece of Wisconsin folklore centers around mastodons. And, though I often try to keep an open mind in writing these chapters, this one is most likely folklore.

In the 1990s, folklorist Dennis Boyer was collecting tales for his new book, eventually to be released as *Giants in the Land: Folktales and Legends of Wisconsin* in 1997. In Richland Center, Wisconsin, at the VFW Post 2267 building in the bar, Boyer was told a real whopper by a man identified only as Scott, claiming to have

---

mastodon," as the bones had come from several different places, not just Boaz!

knowledge of pygmy mastodons roaming Wisconsin!

Probably inspired by the tale of the Boaz Mastodon, the informant claimed that mastodons survived in the area all the way up until the Great Depression. As to why nobody saw the huge creatures, the answer was simple: they had shrunk through micro-evolution! With food sources dwindling, over time the mastodons bred smaller and smaller each year, thus prolonging their food supply with their smaller bellies. Also, due to their smaller stature, they eventually became so tiny that hunting parties of Kickapoo no longer spotted them. Hiding in small caves and hollowed out trees, these dwarf mastodons were all but forgotten.

By the time settlers began arriving in the Wisconsin area, the mastodons were only the size of dogs and cats. Mostly sighted in the Southwestern portion of the state, the largest concentration of them could be found in Richland Center, Wild Rose, and, of course, Boaz. All was well between the mini-mastodons and the Wisconsinites until the Great Depression hit. The small mastodons went from being novelties seen in the wild to being food during the hard times. "The old women did have recipes and the meat was said to taste good," Scott told Boyer.[43] It wasn't just people who turned to hunting the little mammoths, but also starved packs of wild dogs whose masters could no longer feed them. Actually, they got so small that even cats could hunt the poor mastodons. "I even heard of a cat adopting some little ones instead of eating them," Scott added.[44]

By 1943, the pygmy mammoth was all but extinct. As they became rarer and rarer, some people allegedly captured these little creatures not to eat, but to keep as pets. Unfortunately, these mini-mastodons did not breed in captivity and became extinct for good by 1944 (though some claimed a few survived into the 1950s). The teller of the tall tale claimed that he had seen items made from their hides, such as wallets, ashtrays made from their skulls, and even ivory utensils from their tusks! Scott claimed to have seen photos of the creatures and supposedly a taxidermized specimen existed in Nevels Corners. Of course, none of these artifacts have surfaced that anyone knows of...

Sources:

Boyer, Dennis. *Giants in the Land: Folktales and Legends of Wisconsin.* Prairie Oak Press, 1997.

---

[43] Boyer, *Giants in the Land*, p.134.
[44] Ibid.

BABY DINOSAUR TRACKS?

Canyon Lake Mystery Monster

IN JULY OF 2002, torrential flooding in the Canyon Lake region of Texas cut a deep gorge into the landscape. As it turned out, this gorge revealed ancient strata containing—what else?—dinosaur tracks. By 2007, the Parks Service officially named the area Canyon Lake Gorge and began offering tours of the area so that onlookers could see the tracks for themselves. Embedded in limestone and now protected by a large pavilion, the tracks can be viewed at a distance from a walkway encircling the prints. It is believed that the three-toed tracks were made by an acrocanthosaurus around 108 million years ago along an ancient seashore.

Some of Canyon Lake Gorge's dinosaur tracks.
(Canyon Lake Chamber)

However, what may have been a real live dinosaur may have made fresh tracks on the shore of Canyon Lake in the early 1970s. They were found by a well-established resident of the area, Benno J. Rust, who would have been in his mid-fifties to sixties when he found the tracks. His discovery was reported in Roger Nuhn's "Shots at Random" column appearing in the *New Braunfels Herald Zeitung* on February 3, 1972, on page 17:

By Roger Nuhn

MONSTER TRACKS?

MYSTERY MONSTER

The photos of tracks above were taken by Benno Rust up at Canyon Lake, about 30 or 40 feet from the water's edge, at the carcass of a full grown deer which had had its throat torn out.

Apparently the deer had been killed at the water's edge, and then dragged to where Benno found it, and the predator fed on it there. A flattened out place in tall grass nearby indicated that the predator had bedded down there after feeding.

The tracks are reproduced a bit less than half size here, Benno says. They are not cat tracks, since the impression of the claws is clear. Cats walk with their claws retracted-they leave no claw marks They may be coyote tracks, but they appear too long compared to their width and almost web-footed in these photos. One person we showed these photos to without any explanation identified them immediately as dinosaur tracks. Must have been a small dinosaur.

So maybe we've got a Canyon Lake monster to compete with the Loch Ness creature. Keep your eyes open.

Unfortunately, that's where the trail ends for the "Canyon Lake monster," which never became a Nessie-level sensation. But, the mutilated carcass did at least indicate that an unknown predator was stalking the shores of Canyon Lake in 1972, which for now does make it a cryptid if not a "baby dinosaur".

GOLD AND THE BONES
OF A MONSTER
A Cave of Prehistoric Terrors

SINCE THIS SERIES is named "Cowboys & Saurians," it would seem a shame to pass up a story as rich in Western history as this. True, it contains no live monsters, but it does contain the bones of a prehistoric beast that would appear to have lived past its accepted extinction date. And it was found in a cave connected both to a famous lost treasure and a lost lawyer by the name of Albert J. Fountain, who disappeared within New Mexico's White Sands in 1896.

Fountain did so just after presenting evidence to convict Oliver Lee of cattle rustling and many say that's why he disappeared—forever. The mysterious disappearance was the talk of the territory for many years and even lured Pat Garrett—the sheriff who slew Billy the Kid—out of retirement to solve the case. He didn't, and to this day Fountain's body has never been found within the White Sands.

Albert J. Fountain.

Some have tied Fountain's disappearance in with a long lost treasure, the Padre LaRue Mine, said to be located in the vicinity of the White Sands area. Fountain had recently found gold in an undisclosed location which sounded very much to be the old Padre Mine. But he disappeared before he was ever able to move forward on his fabulous find.

After his father's death, Albert Fountain Jr. kept up his father's search for gold in the vicinity of the Organ Mountains near White Sands. Though

Fountain Jr. was never fortunate enough to find the Lost Padre La Rue Mine, he may have found something even more fantastic, though less valuable. Southeast of Las Cruces, at a spot known as Bishop's Cap, Fountain Jr. found gold. Or, rather, Fountain Jr. didn't find it but owned the cave where it was discovered by Benito and Sefino Benavides.

White Sands.
(Historical Society for Southeast New Mexico)

From a story published on March 15, 1929, one could surmise that the brothers were likely searching for the Lost Padre Mine, as it stated: "Recalling stories of buried treasure in this section and thinking that the cave showed evidence of having been artificially closed, another treasure hunt was started which resulted in finding the huge bones of an animal as well as those of human beings." Later, a separate article identified Fountain Jr. as "one of the promoters of the original treasure hunt in the cave." So, perhaps

Fountain hired the Benavides brothers to continue his father's search for the Lost La Rue gold?

Whatever the case, a lengthy article from the July 23, 1930 *Roswell Daily Record* related the excavation of the cave, which turned up far more than gold:

GOLD FOUND IN EXCAVATING ANCIENT RUINS

Las Cruces, July 23—(AP)—Excavations will be resumed in the cave on the east side of Bishops cap, a prominent landmark fifteen miles southeast of Las Cruces, about the first of August, according to Albert J. Fountain Jr., one of the owners of the cave. The work will be under the supervision of geologists sent out from the Los Angeles Museum, together with Roscoe P. Conkling, archaeologist of El Paso.

Though Fountain did not commit himself, it was learned from other sources a small vein of gold has been discovered in the cave, for which the excavations will be resumed.

The cave, found last year by two brothers, Benito and Sefino Benavides while prospecting, has proved to be one of the most startling scientific findings in the southwest.

Recalling the details of buried treasure, the brothers set to work to enlarge the opening. They soon found themselves in a cavern several feet across with a floor sloping downward. Further excavations in the earth accumulations of the cave revealed human bones and the fossilized bones of animals.

They were brought to the attention of Conkling who, realizing the possible importance of the field, reported the find to the Museum of Los Angeles and J.W. Lytle, assistant paleontologist of the institution arrived in short time to take charge of the excavations.

Fossils which had been unearthed at a depth of 10 feet were identified as those of the ground sloth. Excavations in the cave are reported to have brought to light eight feet below where the first human skull was found a hard contacts deposit believed to have been water laid. This is given special significance in view of the fact that 18 inches below the deposit additional human fragments were found indicating that no intrusive human burials had occurred. These facts placed the human bones in definite association with those of the animals regarded as extinct since the Pleistocene period. Midway between the two human skulls, it was said, practically the complete skeleton of a ground sloth was found.

Bones of the extinct horse, camel and sloth have been found in the cave in great numbers it is reported. Dr. William A. Bryan of the Los Angeles Museum also visited the cave and is said to have classed the discoveries as probably some of the most important in America.

It is recalled by old-timers here that tradition places at least one of our numerous "buried treasures" in this vicinity and this is probably the story which led to the discovery of the fossil cave. There is a document still in existence which gives specified instructions for finding "many articles of gold."

Where the story becomes both confusing and more intriguing is when it comes to the dating of the sloth bones in comparison to the human remains. Another newspaper article of the time would seem to imply that it wasn't known that man lived in the Pleistocene Era. *The Alamogordo News* of October 30, 1930, reported:

One of the most interesting addresses, he said, was delivered by Roscoe Conkling, discoverer of the Bishop's Cap cave in the Organ mountains **containing evidence that man lived in the pleistocene age along with the ground sloth, pigmy horse, saber-toothed tiger and other dwellers of earth 25,000 to 100,000 years ago.** Conkling's address was illustrated with many stereopticon slides.

It should be noted that in some circles, Conkling was considered only an amateur archeologist, so perhaps he was unaware that man also lived in the Pleistocene? In any case, even more fossils and fauna were found in the cave not listed in this article, including gnawed human bones from what is thought to be a Dire Wolf den. (Said bones were eventually sent to the Los Angeles Museum and put on display.)

Photo mashup by the author depicting giant sloth chasing Ice Age man across White Sands.

The University of Texas at El Paso seems to have trouble reconciling some of the dates involved in identifying the age of the items in the cave, and they, too, identified Conkling as only a "layman" and "an untrained paleontologist."[45] They said that his report on the cave left much to be desired. The report goes on to detail more ground sloth remains discovered in the area in Aden Fumarole, west-southwest of Las Cruces. The tale is similar to that of well-preserved myolodon remains recovered in South America in the late 1800s. Some felt that the South America specimen in question was exceptionally well-preserved due to the coldness of the cave it was found in, while others believed the animal had died recently. (There had been numerous sightings of creatures resembling giant sloths in South America at the time.)

---

[45] https://www.utep.edu/leb/PleistNM/sites/conklingcavern.htm

Ellis Wright discovering tracks in 1932.
(Courtesy Terri Bunt)

In the case of the Aden Fumarole sloth remains,
they were discovered within some dry guano 100
feet below the entrance to the cave. The specimen
was a nearly complete skeleton with soft tissue

intact on the bones and was thought to be a very recent specimen. How recent? That's where the experts disagree, stating that radiocarbon dating on the dung placed it at 11,080 ± 200 while the preserved hide dated at 9840 ± 160 BP. Due to the discrepancy, it is thought that the hide may have been contaminated by "organic preservatives."[46]

Whatever the case, the White Sands region was rife with prehistoric discoveries in the 1930s. Some even comprised of petroglyphs depicting dinosaurs similar to the Hava Supai canyon petroglyphs of Arizona that also appear to depict at least one dinosaur. Oddly, these dinosaur petroglyphs were mentioned but once in an old article and never discussed again. Better known, and more pertinent to this chapter, was the discovery of some gigantic prints. In the U.S. Department of the Interior booklet, *The Story of the Great White Sands*, it is written:

In the fall of 1932 Ellis Wright, a government trapper, reported that he had found human tracks of unbelievable size imprinted in the gypsum rock on the west side of White Sands. At his suggestion a party was made to investigate. Mr. Wright served as guide, O. Fred Arthur, Supervisor of the Lincoln National Forest, Edgar Cadwalader and one of his sons from Mountain Park, and the writer made up the party. As Mr. Wright had

[46] www.utep.edu/leb/pleistnm/taxaMamm/Nothrotheriops.htm

reported there were 13 tracks crossing a narrow
swag, pretty well out between the mountains
and the sands. Each track was approximately
22 inches long and from 8 to 10 inches wide. It
was the consensus that the tracks were made by
a human being, for the print was perfect and
even the instep plainly marked. However there
was not one in the group who cared to venture
a guess as to when the tracks were made or how
they became of their tremendous size. It is one
of the unsolved mysteries of the Great White
Sands.

Ellis Wright and the giant tracks.
(Courtesy Terri Bunt)

And believe it or not, no one could "venture a
guess" until a full 50 years later. Finally, in 1981, a
group from the New Mexico Bureau of Mines and
Mineral Resources studied the footprints after
being alerted to their existence by archeologist

Peter Eidenbach. The researchers deduced the prints didn't belong to a giant human, but rather a prehistoric mammoth, a prehistoric camel and another unidentified mammal made in the Pleistocene era. Even more recently, it has been determined that the tracks of the "giant" were actually those of a giant sloth being pursued by ice age hunters all along. Who knows, perhaps the tracks were made by one of the same beasts discovered in Bishop's Cap?

NEW MONSTER SEEN

California Now Boasts Huge Serpent at Lake Elsinore.

Lake Elsinore, Cal., Sept. 14.—Lake Elsinore has its "monster," too.

"It would move along near the surface of the water, lazy like, and then all at once would swish that huge tail and dart like lightning half the length of the lake," said C. B. Greenstreet, valley rancher, today.

"I know you think I'm crazy, but I saw it—we all saw it, my wife and two children. Waves as high as the light posts washed on the shore in its wake. We watched it ten minutes, hoping some other motorist would come along so we would have proof. Finally the thing, whatever it was, disappeared near the center of the lake."

C. H. Blake and family, who live on the lake shore, said they saw the mysterious, mammal-like thing last Spring.

Legends tell of the frequent appearance of a monster at a point near the lake center where Indians believe there is a great cavern.

A COUPLE CALIFORNIA NESSIES
Lake Monster Flaps

HISTORICALLY SPEAKING, some of the peak decades for the Loch Ness Monster's popularity were the 1930s and the 1960s. Perhaps, then, it was no coincidence that these decades also tended to be peak years for other lake monsters. Were they copycats created by the press or attention hungry "witnesses"? Or, were lake-bound saurians particularly active during these decades for some reason? Who knows? In any case, in this chapter we will take a brief look at two California Nessie copycats from the thirties and the sixties, starting with Elsie.

Though this article from the September 15, 1934 *Brookfield Argus* claims that a "new monster" was seen, the creature from the depths of Lake Elsinore had been sighted before in 1884. However, being fifty years ago, one could forgive the papers for forgetting.

NEW MONSTER SEEN

California Now Boasts Huge Serpent at Lake Elsinore.

Lake Elsinore, Cal., Sept. 14 —Lake Elsinore has its "monster" too. "It would move along near the surface of the water, lazy like, and then all at once would swish that huge tail and dart like lightning half the length of the lake," said C. B. Greenstreet, valley rancher, today.

"I know you think I'm crazy, but I saw it—we all saw it, my wife and two children. Waves as high as the light posts washed on the shore in its wake. We watched it ten minutes, hoping some other motorist would come along so we would have proof. Finally the thing, whatever it was, disappeared near the center of the lake."

C.H. Blake and family, who live on the lake shore, said they saw the mysterious, mammal-like thing last Spring.

Legends tell of the frequent appearance of a monster at a point near the lake center where Indians believe there is a great cavern.

As I pondered in the chapter's introduction, could it be a little fishy that this sighting occurred around the same time that Nessie-mania was sweeping the world? That's tough to say. What we do know is that the 1884 sighting described the creature as basically looking like a plesiosaur but with a few sea-serpent-like traits, which is encouraging. On a disparaging note as to the monster's credibility, the 1934 article also mentioned the Blake family sighting a mammalian monster the previous spring. This in all likelihood was tied to a report of a prankster setting loose a baby sea lion in the lake in 1932. Whether real or imagined, the monster eventually garnered the nickname of Elsie, just like Nessie.

The monster was seen again thirty odd years later by 1967, when a family boating on the lake saw it. Shades of Nessie, undulating humps swam past them in the water. Only three years later it resurfaced in two separate sightings by the same woman, Bonnie Play. She described it as twelve feet long by three feet wide with humps and a dinosaurian head. At an undisclosed date not too long after, three state park employees saw it about fifty feet from their boat. In this case, they could see spines along the humps.

The mid-90s were also prolific for Elsie. In 1993, a man sighted a large whale-type creature in the lake, while in 1994, a fisherman claimed to have hooked the monster accidentally. In the brief glimpse he got of it, he said that the head reminded him of an alligator. After this, a fiberglass replica of Elsie was created and ran a whopping 103 feet long!

Furthermore, Lake Elsinore appears to be a "window area," or that is a location with a high frequency of paranormal activity like Skinwalker Ranch. In the vicinity are also seen UFOs, ghosts, vampire cults of some kind, and a small group of citizens that all claim to have been reincarnated and knew each other in a past life.

While Lake Elsinore may indeed be a Window Area, there is a problem with the monster due to the fact that the lake has dried out several times since the sightings began (specifically once in 1954). Naturally, no monsters, dead or alive, were found. However, even the 1934 article mentioned the possibility of the monster living within a great cavern, while others put forth the theory that the serpent swam up the San Jacinto River.

More fleeting than Elsie was another serpentine cryptid mentioned in various California-based newspapers in April of 1969. Headlined "COMPETITION FOR LOCH NESS? Odd Beast In Las Gallinas Creek," the article reported "Scientific circles here and in Scotland were all aquiver today at reports that a Loch Ness-type monster had been sighted in Santa Venetia's Las Gallinas Creek."

The article, which is mostly satirical, jokes quite a bit about the Loch Ness Monster but does offer the honest accounts of the witnesses, which described the monster as being eight feet long with a luminous tail. It was sighted in the first week of April by a man named Fred Ullner from his dock. Around the same time, Ullner and his neighbor, identified only as Mrs. William Thompson, saw it as it poked its head out of the water. "I'd never seen anything quite like the wake it was leaving," she told the press. A bit later, she saw it leave the water and come onto land, heading into some bullrushes. "I couldn't have told you whether it had eight legs or none," she said.

THE MONSTER
As describeed to I-J artist
Jack Lucey

Illustration of the Monster in the papers.

Both the witnesses concurred that the monster's head was four to five inches thick, and that the body was four inches thick best that they could

259

tell. The luminous tail, they said, was about two feet long. Despite the luminous tail, one expert put forth the theory that the beast was simply an escaped boa constrictor.

Apparently, that was the last major sighting of the creature. A monster watch on April 18th failed to yield any results, and some theorized that the water was "too rough for the monsters that day."

CAVE OF THE THUNDERBIRD
The Treasure Hunter's Tale

ONE OF THE GREATEST folklorists of our time is undoubtedly W.C. Jameson. From what I can tell, he's the only source for the following tale, which appeared in his book *Unsolved Mysteries of the Old West*. This one is especially good as it features lost Spanish gold within the cave of a monster, a Thunderbird to be exact.

Sometime in the early 1980s, a treasure hunter of Native American descent was in southeastern Utah when he was told a fabulous tale about a procession of Spanish conquistadors attacked by the Ute tribe around the year 1738. The conquistadors were leading a pack train of about 30 mules transporting silver ingots mined in

Colorado down to Mexico City. In a narrow canyon, the Ute massacred the trespassers going through their land. Two Spaniards escaped their notice and fled to an outcrop of rocks at a nearby slope. There the two men watched in horror as their comrades were scalped and cut to pieces. Then the Ute did something very unusual: they began leading the burros up a narrow path along the cliffside. While it would make sense for most people to take the treasure somewhere safe, many Native American tribes care little for silver or gold. The purpose of the trek wasn't to hide the silver as it turned out; it was to make an offering to a monster.

The two Spaniards watched in confusion as the Ute led the burrows into a cave in the cliff face. As they did so, they passed under a huge depiction of a bird-like monster etched on the cliff wall. Then, from inside the cave, the men could hear the mules crying out as the Ute slashed their throats to leave them there dead. But why? After the Ute departed, the two Spaniards entered the cave to find that not only had the burros' throats been cut, but for some reason, their hooves had been removed. The two men, unable to transport the large amounts of silver, trekked back to Mexico City empty-handed and related the tale to officials of the Catholic Church.

This was the story told to Jameson's unnamed treasure hunter, who used the vague directions given to him by the teller to track down the cave. Traveling through spookily named locales such as Devil's Canyon, Goblin Valley, and Hoodoo

Arch, miraculously, the man found the lost cave of the Thunderbird. According to Jameson, the Thunderbird painting he saw seemed to resemble a pterodactyl, as it sported a reptilian tail, while the head featured something akin to a horn or a crest. In a way, it sounded similar to the Piasa Bird of Illinois, pictured below.

While this was certainly an interesting find, the treasure hunter was still more concerned with the lost silver, obscured somewhere inside the cave by several centuries worth of fine sand blown in by the wind. Over three months, the dedicated hunter excavated the cave taking out one bucketful of sand at a time. One day, as if to confirm the tale of the pack mules, in a sand bucket he found what looked to be the hoof of a burro. That was only the beginning, though. Soon he began finding burro bones as well. He anticipated finding the lost silver any day. Instead, he found something more startling.

One day while taking a rest, the man noticed the shaft of a huge feather protruding from the sand. And by huge, he meant as thick as one of his fingers and over 18 inches long. Obviously, this wasn't the feather of any normal hawk or eagle. He took the feather to several experienced ornithologists who found that it was most comparable to an eagle feather, just much too large to be any normal eagle. Each of the experts felt that it could only belong to a heretofore undiscovered avian species.

As for the treasure hunter, he continued his search for silver only to find more burro bones and giant feathers. Eventually he was forced to depart on other business without ever finding his silver. However, for cryptozoologists, the strange feathers would be far more valuable than silver or gold...

Sources:

Jameson, W.C. *Unsolved Mysteries of the Old West.* Taylor Trade Publishing, 2012.

THE WHITE RIVER MONSTER
Southern Saurian Hunt

"WELCOME TO JACKSONPORT, Home of the White River Monster," a sign proudly proclaims in the small Arkansas town located along the White River. Sightings of a monster there began in 1915 when a woman from Little Rock claimed to have seen a large creature swimming in the White River. Supposedly, before that, Native American legends also referred to the monster. But, most interesting of all, folklore even tells that the monster took part in the Civil War. Specifically, it was rumored that the creature was responsible for overturning a Confederate gunboat in White River. Yet more stories say that it capsized other boats in the river, and yet another account had soldiers shooting at it from the riverbanks.

White River Postcard.

Whether those stories actually happened or not, the sightings peaked in the depression era of the 1930s when four men signed an affidavit swearing they had seen the monster. One of the men, a farmer named Bramblett Bateman, said in his affidavit that on July 1, 1937, at one o'clock, he saw an object about 12 feet long and four to five feet wide break the surface of the river.

During his July sighting, Bateman had called the sheriff's office to request a high-powered rifle so that he could kill the monster. The sheriff's office obliged and sent several law officers to the river, among them Z.B. Reid, who would later make his own sworn affidavit concerning the monster. According to Reid, he and several other men watched the river for several hours and when they were finally ready to go home, the monster showed. Reid caught a glimpse of it and said it reminded him of a giant sturgeon or catfish.

As often happens with sightings like these in small towns the newswires picked up on the story and other witnesses soon came forward. Ethel Smith of Little Rock said that she had seen it in 1924 and described it as having grey skin and making loud blowing noises. Soon several others came forward with earlier sightings that also matched these descriptions. In a predictable pattern, media interest grew and efforts were intensified to find the monster. One of the first articles that I could find on the fiasco was published on July 12, 1937, in the *Danville Bee*:

RIVER 'MONSTER' ATTRACTS THRONGS

Sightseers Wait in Vain as Creature Only Snorts Bubbles From Depths

NEWPORT, Ark. July 12—(AP)—Newport residents schemed today to trap a mysterious "monster" that snorted bubbles from the 60-foot depths of a White river eddy six miles south of here as hundreds of sightseers who waited in vain for him to break the surface.

Belief that the "monster" is a fish of enormous size—possibly an alligator gar or sturgeon—was strengthened by the assertion of Capt. Jack Carter of the U.S. snagboat Tom Stallings that the bubbles were "certainly caused by some living object."

Skeptics previously advanced the theory that the "monster" was a sunken scow forced upward from time to time by gas from decaying leaves on the river bottom and shifting currents.

Bramlett Bateman, plantation owner; J.L. Defries, farmer; Dee Wyatt, a negro farmer and his wife, Sylvia, asserted they had seen the mysterious creature on more than one occasion. They expressed belief it is a fish.

Their stories were told and retold yesterday to Sunday crowds who drove here from several states to watch for the "monster." Country roads made almost impassable by rain kept other hundreds from the bank of the stream. A newsreel camera man was among the disappointed.

The bubbles came up along side a launch occupied by Captain Carter and 12 others. His snagboat is on its way downstream now and will reach the eddy sometime this week.

W. E. Penix, Newport, said he planned to construct a huge net to drag the eddy in hopes of snaring the "monster." Fenix said he had no expectation of landing the creature with a net but believed he might entangle it long enough for it to be definitely identified.

Next, the *Galveston Daily* News of July 18, 1937 reported:

DIVER TO SOLVE RIVER MONSTER MYSTERY HIRED

ALL DRESSED UP TO CAPTURE "MONSTER"

Deep Sea Diver Charles B. Brown, with trusty eight-foot harpoon in hand, shown yesterday as he was about to dive for the White River "monster" near Newport, Ark. Last reports were to the effect that he failed to find any monster on the river's bottom.

Newport, Ark., July 17—AP—A former navy diver will attempt next week to solve the mystery of Newport's White River "monster." Marion Dickens, president of the Chamber of Commerce, today said arrangements had been made with the diver, C. E. Brown, now employed by the United States engineers, to explore the eddy six miles south of here.

Dee Wyatt, a negro farmer living on the eddy bank, reported he saw the "monster" again today. Wyatt reiterated his previous claims that it was something of enormous size that came to the top of the water briefly and then sank again.

Skeptics insisted the "monster" was an old scow, forced upward from time to time by shifting currants or river gases...

Dickens said the diver was being employed to spike reports that the "monster" story was a fiction invented by the Chamber of Commerce as a publicity stunt.

Diver Begins Search For River Monster

MEMPHIS, Tenn., July 19 (U.P)—C. B. Brown, diver employed by the U. S. Engineering Corps, today prepaired to go to Newport, Ark., to search for a "White River monster."

The so-called monster was reported by white and negro residents of the river section to be a "slick, slimy thing as big as a box car." They said the "monster" occasionally came to the surface.

Veteran fishermen chuckled and called the "monster a monstrous good fish story."

Brown was hired by the Newport Chamber of Commerce. The diver was uncertain when he would start the search.

Amarillo Daily News (July 20, 1937).

On July 20, the *Hope Star* explained:

Memphis Diver to Harpoon Monster

Will Make Search of White River Bottom at
Newport Thursday

MEMPHIS. Tenn. Diver Charles B. Brown
will "harpoon" Arkansas' White river
"monster" if he encounters the mysterious
"something" in a diving search of the river eddy
six miles south of Newport, Ark., Thursday.

"I'm going to take a harpoon with me which
I'll tie to the barge," the U.S. engineers
professional diver said. "If I run across this
monster I'm going to let him have it with the
harpoon and get out of there as fast as I can."

However, Brown reiterated his belief the
monster is nothing but "a large catfish."

The Newport Chamber of Commerce
engaged Brown for the search to "get to the
bottom" of the mystery, subject of considerable
speculation since a farmer reported sighting the
creature three weeks ago.

On the 22nd, this article outlined the media
frenzy the search was causing.

**Business Is Suspended at Newport, Ark.,
As Deep Sea Diver Hunts River 'Monster'
Area of About 50 Foot Square Explored
Without Trace of Mystery Animal; Crowds
Flock to Scene of Four-Day Quest**

NEWPORT, Ark., July 22.— (AP)—Business was virtually suspended here today as hundreds of Newport residents and tourists watched deep sea diver Charles B. Brown of Memphis begin a hunt for White river's mysterious "monster."

Holiday atmosphere prevailed at the scene six miles to the south as Brown twice invaded a mile-long, 60-foot-deep eddy where a huge bubble-blowing denizen of the river was reported sighted several times in the past four weeks.

An eight-foot, razor-keen harpoon in hand, Brown first was lowered into the water in a test exploration. This afternoon he began his four-day hunt in earnest.

The Newport Chamber of Commerce sponsored the search after reports the monster story was created to obtain publicity for this farming town of 4,347 inhabitants.

Newport stores closed and crowds flocked to the scene for what may turn out to be an epochal discovery or just a sunken boat or oil tank.

Half a dozen eye-witnesses including Bramlett Bateman, plantation owner, reported seeing a great creature rise to the surface on rare intervals, float silently for a few minutes and then submerge.

Brown formerly dived for the U. S. navy and now is employed by the U. S. engineers. He said he expected to find "an overgrown catfish." Others have theorized the monster was only an old scow or an alligator gar.

A dance floor was constructed near the eddy with announcement an orchestra would play for dancers as long as the hunt lasted. The chamber of commerce fixed a small fee for spectators to defray Brown's expenses.

Brown explored an area about 50 foot square today. After spending two hours and 40 minutes under water, he said he found no clue to the stream's "monster" mystery.

Brown said he found no overturned boat or undercurrent of air that would send bubbles to the surface.

Persons who have reported seeing the marine creature said it had made its presence known by sending up occasional bubbles from the bottom.

Spectators at the scene were from Arkansas, Mississippi, Missouri and Tennessee.

However, by July 24th, the *Blytheville Courrier News* reported that the jig was up:

DIVER GIVES UP MONSTER SEARCH
Admissions To Newport Show Fall Off; Charles Brown Disgusted

NEWPORT, Ark., July 24. <UP> Charles Brown, U.S. engineers deep sea diver, today gave up in disgust after giving the White river monster three chances to come out and fight fair. Muddy water suspected by some as being nothing but pure meanness on the part of the monster prevented Brown from getting a good view of what was under the water at the bend in White river where a monster "as big as a boxcar" is supposed to repose.

Another cause for discontinuance of the dives might have been that paid admissions became too few, Brown was named winner by default, proving to a large degree man's superiority over his fellow mammal, the sea monster.

DIVER GIVES UP MONSTER SEARCH

Admissions To Newport Show Fall Off; Charles Brown Disgusted

NEWPORT, Ark., July 24. (UP) —Charles Brown, U. S. engineers deep sea diver, today gave up in disgust after giving the White river monster three chances to come out and fight fair. Muddy water—suspected by some as being nothing but pure meanness on the part of the monster—prevented Brown from getting a good view of what was under the water at the bend in White river where a monster "as big as a boxcar" is supposed to repose.

Another cause for discontinuance of the dives might have been that paid admissions became too few. Brown was named winner by default, proving to a large degree man's superiority over his fellow mammal, the sea monster.

The July 25th *Ada Evening News* also reported on the failure.

Hunt For River Monster Closed
Theory Is Developed That White River
"Something" Leaves Hole

NEWPORT. Ark. July 24.—
Maybe the "White River Monster" —if ever a monster there was—just could not take it.

An underwater hunt for the mysterious "something" which several local residents declared they have seen rising to the surface of the river with a prodigious snort, was abandoned today.

Those who still retained faith in the existence of a "monster" were quick to theorize that so much hub-bub on the river bank had frightened the monster away.

With a band blaring from a hastily erected dance-hall beside the river, sight-seeing planes zooming over the stream, and concessionaires hawking their offerings, it was easy for them to believe the poor fish had sought quieter and more congenial haunts in lower reaches of the river.

Side attractions to the "monster-hunt" did a land-office business this week among the thousands attracted to the scene. There were still crowds on hand today, despite the announcement of Professional Diver C. B. Brown that he would not again go down to the river bed, harpoon armed to meet the monster.

An accident to an air valve, and heavy rains which increased the murkiness of the water and the driftwood in the stream led to Brown's decision. He said, however, he was convinced the "monster" was actually an overgrown fish, although he never encountered it, and not a sunken log or scow as some believed.

His explorations were sponsored by the chamber of commerce to refute charges the tale of the "monster" was a local publicity stunt.

Gar Nine Feet Long Caught

MOUNTAIN HOME, Ark., Jan. 18 (U.P.)—A 220-pound gar, which may have been the "White River Monster" that fishermen reported seeing two years ago, was on display at a meat market here today.

The gar, nine feet long and a foot wide across the head, was caught in a branch of the White River by two fishermen. After a furious fight they got it into shallow water and killed it.

Despite the creature being written off in the press, Bateman claimed to see the monster months later in September, roughly 200 yards from where he saw it last. Four years later, there was a resurgence of interest in the monster tale in 1940. *The Amarillo Globe* of January 18, 1940, reported that a nine-foot-long gar caught in the river was really the monster all along. This, in turn, seemed to prompt yet another theory as to the monster's legitimacy from a story in the *Jefferson City Daily Capital News* on February 24, 1940:

White River 'Monster' Seen As Device of Shell Digger

LITTLE ROCK. Ark., Feb. 23 — (AP) — Belief that a "monster" which appeared in White River near Newport in 1937 to cause tremendous excitement in those parts was an ingenious device of a shell digger to frighten competitors away from a bed of valuable mussel shells was expressed today by a state game and fish commission official.

Commission Secretary D. N. Graves said he had received a report that the "monster" was an overturned scow which the owner and discoverer of the bed of shells submerged or brought to the surface at will through a complicated set of wires while he hid behind bushes on the bank.

"The story has the ring of truth and I am convinced it is true," said Graves, who three years ago discounted the "monster" story while thousands gathered on the banks of the White to get a view of it—which in most cases they didn't.

Here's the story as given to Graves by the operator of a Newport filling station, who said the owner of the "monster" had related it to him:

An old shell digger found a bed of shells in a river sandbank in shallow water. They were of a type more valuable than ordinary mussel shells, Graves reporting they were shells which European manufacturing companies buy to make knife handles, ear rings and other novelties.

Elated but afraid that other "shell" men would muscle in on his mussel discovery, the old man overturned his scow, then hitched to it a set of wires. At one end, under the water, they were attached to roots of a tree. At the other they led to the hiding spot on the bank.

"The story goes that the old man started the tale of a monster in the river himself," Graves said. "When one or two persons would come down there, he would get in the bushes and pull the "monster" up for a few minutes. But if a crowd was on hand, the "monster" didn't appear because the shell digger was afraid he would be discovered.

"The story spread and within a few days people from four or five states were in Newport to get a look. News and movie camera men appeared overnight. A professional diver was brought in to make an underwater search and the owner of land along the river bank did a land office business charging admission.

"All this time, the old man was working busily at night digging his shells. Due to the crowds, the situation got clear out of hand so one night he slipped out and cut the wires, letting the "monster" ramble on down the river. By that time he had completed digging the shells."

Graves said he considered significant a description given by the few who saw the "monster" that it had "hide like a wet elephant." asserting that the moss-covered bottom of a scow would have this appearance.

"There's also corroboration in that the 'monster' stayed under water when a crowd was on the bank," Graves added, "also in the fact that it disappeared altogether after about two weeks."

That's all good and well, but it can't explain further sightings to occur years later. Actually, going back to Brown's 1937 dive, shouldn't he have stumbled across this sunken boat? One of the articles specifically noted that "Brown said he found no overturned boat or undercurrent of air that would send bubbles to the surface."

Perhaps the monster left that portion of the White River for a time only to return a few decades later. Starting in 1966, three people out fishing described a mystery creature that had a tail they likened to a mermaid. Actually, maybe this one was a mermaid since they said it also had arm-like flippers and a quasi-humanoid head like a monkey! That strange, one-off sighting aside, a true renaissance for the monster occurred in the 1970s wherein a photo of the animal was snapped and published in a newspaper.

The White River Monster photo from 1972 by
Cloyce Warren.

During this flap of sightings in the summer of
1971 quite a few people saw the monster. In June,
Ernest Denks saw the creature, which he
described as looking more like an animal than a
fish and having a bonelike protrusion coming
from its forehead. In the next sighting, Cloyce
Warren captured a photo of the monster while
fishing with some friends. The evidence became
more interesting when 14x8 inch tracks of the
monster were found on Towhead Island in the
riverbed of which plaster casts were made by the
police department. The tracks were three towed
with claws. More were found later, along with
flattened trees and grass.

The Towhead Island tracks inspired a local trapper, Ollie Ritcherson, and a 13-year-old boy, Joey Dupree, to take a boat out to the island. They were not to be disappointed. Although they didn't see the monster, they collided with it in their boat, lifting them up onto the creature's back for a few brief moments.

After that there would be only one more sighting of the monster that year by a man named Jim Gates, who observed the creature thrashing about in the water for a full 15 minutes. In 1972 a vacationing family saw the cryptid near Jacksonport Park and estimated what they saw to be nearly 60 to 75 feet long. That is considerably larger than any previous sightings, which were only about 20 feet at the most. R.C. McClauglen, the father of the group, said he could discern some sort of head and a spiny backbone. That was the last recorded sighting of the White River Monster.

After an extensive investigation of the sightings, Dr. Roy P. Mackal came to the conclusion that the White River Monster was likely an elephant seal. His reasoning for this was that one had likely gotten into the Mississippi River and then trailed off into the White River. Also, witnesses described behavior similar to an elephant seal, such as the loud bellowing noises as well as its surfacing patterns and skin texture/color. The boney protrusion described by Ernest Denks could be attributed to an elephant seal's protruding nose and "trunk."

On the other hand, if one wants to be skeptical of Mackal's theory, one can. Some witnesses distinctly described the monster as serpent-like and the grainy photograph by Cloyce Warren does appear to show a spiny back of some sort, leading one to wonder how an elephant seal could have such an appearance. Also, as stated before, accounts of the cryptid go back much further than the 1930s to the time of the Native Americans of the area.[47]

Monster or seal, nearby towns like to capitalize on the creature nonetheless. During Christmas time the White River Monster, called "Whitey" by the locals, is the lead float in their annual Christmas parade in Jacksonport. Although Jacksonport has no festival for their monster, it does have the distinction of having its own official refuge, the "White River Monster Refuge," where harming the creature is illegal, deemed so by Senator Robert Harvey in February of 1973.

---

[47] That is, unless these "earlier" stories were made up in the 1930s.

POSTSCRIPT

DEATH VALLEY'S LOST
CITY OF THE DINOSAURS

A FEW YEARS AGO, back when I was capping off the first *Cowboys & Saurians* book, I remember struggling with just how to end the tome. Since that first volume had been partially inspired by *The Valley of Gwangi*, Ray Harryhausen's beloved cowboys vs. dinosaur movie from 1969, I decided to close the book with an entry on a location similar to the aforementioned "Valley of Gwangi." In that case, while I found no Mexican deserts inhabited by an Allosaurus, I did find a lost plateau in the Grand Canyon rumored to be inhabited by a prehistoric horse known as the Eohippus. The Eohippus, or dawn horse, played a large role in the film though it was often overshadowed by the dinosaurs. Still, I was intrigued to have found a historical precursor to the movie. On the next book,

Cowboys & Saurians: Ice Age, I discovered what appeared to be the real-life inspiration for Edgar Rice Burroughs's *Land That Time Forgot,* hidden along the icy tundra. Then, of course, *Cowboys & Saurians South of the Border* was easy to cap off as Sir Arthur Conan Doyle had based T*he Lost World* on real reports of dinosaurs running wild in South America.

Death Valley by Ansel Adams.

While I can find no real location that lines up with any significant films to close out this book, there was still one place that stuck out to me: Death Valley. After all, Death Valley did serve as the backdrop for several classic monster movies, chief among them 1954's *Them!* Death Valley also takes us back to the first book in this series, which included an entry on the mostly forgotten "Dragon of Death Valley."

Iguanodon Depiction from the 19th Century.

Published in various papers throughout the spring of 1892 were reports of a dinosaur-like creature in Death Valley. The creature was likened to an Iguanodon, then a popular variety of dinosaur, by the papers and described as thirty feet long and different "from any of the known forms of the present epoch." The paper reported that the Death Valley dragon was

> ...an immense monster, walking part of the time on its hind feet and at times dragging itself through the sand and leaving tracks of a three-toed foot and a peculiar scratchy configuration in the sand whenever it changed its form of locomotion and dragged itself.

The forelimbs of the animal were extremely short and it occasionally grasped the nearest scrub and devoured it. The thumb of the three-pronged forefoot was evidently a strong, conical spine that would be a dangerous weapon of attack. Whenever the animal stood upright it was fully fourteen feet high.

The head was as large as a good-sized cask and was shaped somewhat like a horse, while the body was as large as that of an elephant, with a long tail extending from the hindquarters something like that of an alligator.

Interestingly, the witness observed the monster at the "edge of a great sinkhole of alkaline water" that "my guides told me was a bottomless pit." This locale was most likely Devil's Hole, a geothermal pool with waters that keep a near-constant salinity and temperature of 92 °F or 33 °C. Considering the bottom has yet to be found, it's the perfect place for a monster.

It also lines right up with the explanations given for surviving dinosaurs in 1950's era B-movies, where some bespectacled scientist would claim the remnant dinosaur survived extinction by hiding underground. Actually, the Death Valley Expedition of the U.S. biological survey in 1891 did discover a rare, new species of pupfish called *Cyprinodon diabolis*[48] at Devil's hole. So, in 1892,

---

[48] These pupfish became the world's first endangered species as a matter of fact. It is one of the rarest species of fish in the world and only one hundred or so exist at a time

at the time the article was written, the idea of
discovering new, unique animal life in Death
Valley could have easily seeped into the
imagination of a late 19th-century reporter.

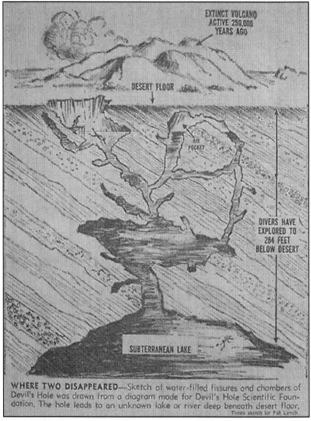

EXTINCT VOLCANO
ACTIVE 250,000
YEARS AGO

DESERT FLOOR

AIR
POCKET

DIVERS HAVE
EXPLORED TO
284 FEET
BELOW DESERT

SUBTERRANEAN LAKE

WHERE TWO DISAPPEARED—Sketch of water-filled fissures and chambers of
Devil's Hole was drawn from a diagram made for Devil's Hole Scientific Foun-
dation. The hole leads to an unknown lake or river deep beneath desert floor.
Times sketch by Pat Lynch

1965 Newspaper Illustration of Devil's Hole.
(Jim Houtz Collection)

within Devil's Hole, again, the only place in the world where
they are found.

Regardless of the unique properties of Devil's Hole, I initially wrote off the Death Valley dinosaur tale as a true "Snaik Story," or a made-up tale that deserved to be forgotten in the annals of remnant dinosaurs. And perhaps it should be. However, I recently found another Death Valley dinosaur tale, this one conjoined with a lost city buried beneath the sands that made me wonder if there might be some truth to the 1892 story yet.

In the 1920s, a man named White was looking through an old abandoned mine at Wingate Pass in the southwest corner of Death Valley. Suddenly, the floor collapsed and he fell into an underground tunnel. With no other choice, White explored the labyrinth before him and eventually stumbled upon a catacomb of mummies. According to White, there were hundreds of them, all clad in leather and surrounded by gold bars and other treasures.

Odder yet, White saw a tunnel that was lit by a pale, green and yellow-tinted light. Afraid of the strange light source, he elected not to go towards it alone and, somehow, White made his way back to the surface. White's bold claim was backed by a Paiute named Tom Wilson, a local guide and trapper in the area who said that his grandfather had discovered the catacombs many years ago. His story was mostly the same as White's, claiming that his grandfather wandered through miles and miles of tunnels. Only in the grandfather's case, the people in the underground city still lived. They were fair-skinned and wore leather-like clothing just as White described the mummies. They spoke in a tongue unknown to the Paiute, and curiously, they also had horses underground and an unknown food source he'd never seen on the surface.

Upon returning to the surface, no one believed the man's far-out tale, which was why Wilson was happy to hear the account of White. Eventually, Wilson and White connected, and the latter agreed to lead a team of archeologists to the underground city. However, as is usual in these types of stories, White was unable to locate the exact entrance again despite having been there three times before. Instead, they found only a dead-end tunnel carved through a section of solid rock. Wilson would then spend the rest of his life searching for the entrance.[49]

While that may put a dampener on the legend of the lost city, in 1932, yet another similar tale emerged in the book *Death Valley Men* by Bourke Lee, an old area prospector. He, too, told of an underground city, this one located in the Panamint Mountains of Death Valley. According to Lee, two men identified only as Bill and Jack were exploring the area of Wingate Pass. The ground suddenly collapsed and they fell into an old mine shaft and from there followed it for 20 miles into the heart of the Panamint Mountains.

In the men's own words, which appear in *Death Valley Men*, they described it as a "city thousands of-years-old and worth billions of dollars!"[50]

---

[49] He passed away in 1968.

[50] Reprinted in *Lost Cities & Ancient Mysteries of the Southwest*, p.470.

The underground city they found sounded very similar to the one described by White. If it wasn't the same one, then it must've been a sister city. They found mummies within the city that they said wore large armbands and carried golden spears. There were also treasure chambers within stone vaults full of gold bars and statues, along with precious gemstones.

The two men grabbed all the treasure they could carry and then found an exit tunnel leading upwards and out halfway up the eastern slope of the Panamint Mountains. Sadly, similar to the conclusion of White's tale, when the men tried to find the entrance a second time, they failed.[51] So, in the end, they had no proof of their fantastic tale. Ultimately, the two men disappeared on one of their expeditions into the mountains to find the exit they had used.

Finally, in the late 1940s came one of the most publicized accounts of the lost city yet in the *Butte Montana Standard* on August 5, 1947. It told how a retired Ohio doctor, Dr. F. Bruce Russell, had discovered a mysterious section of caves back in 1931 while sinking a shaft for a mine. Within the caves he saw "relics of an ancient civilization, whose men were eight or nine feet tall, in the Colorado desert near the Arizona-Nevada-California line." The article went on to claim that some of the giant mummies "were taken Sunday from caverns in an area roughly 180 miles square

---

[51] They claimed that a rainstorm had altered the terrain too much to find it.

extending through much of southern Nevada from Death Valley. Calif., across the Colorado river into Arizona."

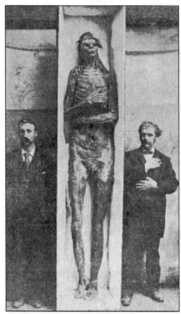

Another giant California mummy
discovered in the 1890s.

However, that wasn't all. In addition to the giant humans were also found giants of another kind: dinosaurs. A separate article printed in the *Valparaiso Vidette Messenger* on August 5, 1947, claimed that in one of the cavernous rooms were the "well-preserved remains of dinosaurs, saber-toothed tigers, imperial elephants and other extinct beasts ... paired off in niches as if on display."

Furthermore, it was also implied that the giants were clothed in the skins of prehistoric animals, as the previous article had also stated that,

"These giants are clothed in garments consisting of a medium length jacket and troupers extending slightly below the knees," said Hill.

"The texture of the material is said to resemble gray dyed sheepskin, but obviously it was taken from an animal unknown today."

Of course, experts were skeptical of the dinosaur claims, with one of the articles stating that "Los Angeles county museum scientists pointed out that dinosaurs and tigers, which Hill said lay side by side in the caves, appeared on earth 10,000,000 to 15,000,000 years apart."

However, these weren't the only prehistoric remains discovered in Death Valley. Long before that, back in 1898, H. Flagler Cowden and his brother Charles were conducting an archaeological dig in Death Valley when they uncovered the skeletal remains of a woman seven and a half feet tall. In the same strata that she was found were also discovered petrified palm trees, other plant life, and the remains of ice age creatures like prehistoric camels and possibly woolly mammoths. Odder yet, the giant mummy appeared to have possessed what may have once been a tail!

Unfortunately, there's not much in the way of follow-ups to the 1947 articles or the lost city beneath Death Valley. For instance, the cave's discoverer, Dr. Russell, died not long after the article's publication when his car was found abandoned with a busted radiator in a remote region of Death Valley. Furthermore, today the area of the alleged underground city near Wingate Pass is part of the China Lake Naval Weapons Center and is closed to the public. Coincidence? Who knows? But, one has to wonder, if the story was actually true, and the city contained the remains of relic dinosaurs, could they have been connected with the creature seen at Devil's Hole in 1892? Devil's Hole is undeniably a strange place for more reasons than just the rare pupfish or the alleged Iguanodon.

In 1965 four high school students went scuba diving into the hole. Two of them never resurfaced from what the papers called a "mysterious fossil water portal". No bodies were ever found. All that turned up was a diving mask, a snorkel, and a flashlight tied to a ledge 100 feet below the surface. Some conspiracy theorists even theorized the hole was an underwater portal to another dimension or time period—perhaps the prehistoric past.

That same decade, Charles Manson also became infatuated with Devil's Hole, thinking it was literally a portal to the underworld. The famous cult leader had left San Francisco for Los Angeles in the late 1960s to come nearer to Death Valley, specifically to be nearer Devil's Hole National Park. Manson had ideas of starting a race war that he codenamed "helter-skelter." Manson would then lead a selected group of whites into the desert where they would multiply in numbers. They would then escape into the underworld, which Manson believed the gateway to was located in the form of Devil's Hole. Beneath that, he would find a sea of gold which was rumored to exist by the Native American population, along with the proverbial land full of milk and honey and a tree that bore 12 different kinds of fruit and which was bathed in eternal light via glowing walls. Furthermore, Manson believed there were already people waiting for him in the underworld. Of course, Manson was arrested before he could make his journey into the underworld but reports do say that he and his followers spent days and days in the heat of Death Valley looking for the entrance in 1968.

Charles Manson, lost treasures, ancient cities, giants, and, most importantly, dinosaurs. Are they all connected in some way besides the strange window area they seem to inhabit? Is there any meaningful way to tie them all together neatly into a bow? Most likely not, but like all the other stories in this book, they add up to one hell of a mystery.

Sources:

Childress, David Hatcher. *Lost Cities and Ancient Mysteries of the Southwest.* Adventures Unlimited Press, 2009.

APPENDIX
EXTRA JERSEY DEVIL ARTICLES

As I stated in the chapter devoted to the Jersey Devil, there were so many articles on the beast published back in 1909 that they could fill their own book. Here are a few more of the ones I came across.

SAW THE WHAT-IS-IT

MOORES TOWN, N.J., Jan. 20.-While nearly all the other South Jersey towns have been seeing the peculiar tracks of the "Leed's Devil," or by whatever name the "what-is-it" may be known, Moorestown residents have been busy trying to ascertain the identity of this most peculiar animal. To a certain extent they have been successful.

Last night John Smith, of near Maple Shade, came into town and told of seeing a strange animal near Mt. Carmel Cemetery. He tried to capture it, but was unsuccessful, the animal disappearing in a nearby gravel pit.

George Snyder, of Maple Shade, also reported having seen the animal while fishing for snappers, and says he could have captured it had not the ice broken with him as he gave chase.

Both descriptions of the animal tally. It is said to be about three feet high, with long black hair covering its entire body. Its arms and hands resemble those of a monkey, but its face is shaped more like that of a dog. Its hoofs are split, and its tail is about a foot long.

The tracks were first seen here early Sunday morning, with new and fresh ones appearing each day. Last night it visited the home of Walter Moore, on East Main street, and was also at a number of homes on Central avenue, cutting itself on a broken bottle at one place, and leaving blood marks in the snow wherever it stepped.

On January 21, on page one of the *Chester Times* came another story about the devil:

FREAK ANIMAL AND ITS TRACKS
many evidences of the visit to Chester of the New Jersey creature with hoofs and wings
IT TAKES LONG STRIDES remarkable leaps, flights were jumps of a two legged monstrosity that has not been seen, but which leaves in its wake peculiar footprints that puzzle the naturalist.

"Whatever kind of animal beast or bird it is I am sure that the theory, that it has wings is correct," said Nat Thompson of the Chester enameling company, at 15th and Esrey streets, yesterday afternoon. He was referring to the strange hoof prints which have been discovered in two states and have stirred up the people to a point of great fear for the safety of their children and their property in the way of fowls.

Mr. Thompson has evidence sufficient to prove to any human being that his theory that the strange thing is a flying machine is correct. He pointed out to the times representative the hoof prints in the snow about composition houses in connection with his plant, and their sudden disappearance, and their reappearance just over the fence of the Chester rural cemetery giving the impression that wings had carried it through space for a distance of about 500 yards.

Mr. Thompson thought nothing of the strange animal when he read about it in the papers yesterday, but when he went outside of his home at 20th and Edgemont Avenue and found imprints on the frozen crust of snow in the rear yard, he was convinced that indeed some stranger had made its appearance in the city. The idea was further confirmed when all of his neighbors found similar footprints in their yards.

A two legged animal

Curiosity prompted him to hunt for the imprints upon the frozen snow when he reached the works, and there in large numbers were the same imprints. A search revealed that the imprints were all about the mill and other buildings, and the singular thing about them is they are all nearly alike, resembling the imprint left by the hoof of a burro.

A diligent search was made but nothing could be seen of the "strange animal" which could walk and fly, and apparently had but two legs. The imprints upon the frozen snow were so large that the people in the upper section of the city at once became very much frightened for fear that it might be an emissary from Hades sent there to carry off children. The women folks are much excited and are guarding their children and chicken coops with great care. There was talk yesterday of citizens forming themselves into a posse to lie in wait and hopes that the maker of the strange hoof prints upon the snow would return, and at least they would get a view of it, if not an opportunity to capture it.

The marks of the hoof are sharply defined, where the snow was soft and then became frozen. Some of the imprints on the property of the Chester enameling company would indicate that in addition to having a hoof, resembling that of a burro, that on the front part, claws appear. These marks are well defined in many places where the sun did not reach the snow yesterday. Many of the marks were obliterated by the strong sun, but enough remain to convince the people of the upper section of the city that a stranger of an unknown character is in their midst.

Unlike the New Jersey towns where this strange animal has made its appearance, no marks of its presence has been found upon the main thoroughfares, but all of them in places which are not frequented at night by many persons. The watchmen at the enamel works intends to keep a close watch for this mysterious animal.

The news was slow in getting into the papers from the New Jersey towns by reason of the fact that the applejack season is at its height. But this condition does not exist in Chester and the appearance of this oddity in Chester and other places has given rise to a great fear.

A hairy proposition

A story reached this city from one of the New Jersey towns yesterday that the animal has hair like an opossum, but there is no evidence in the city as to whether it has or not. The hair story was given credence for the reason that a colored individual of one of the towns found here on the porch floor of one of the residences where the hoof prints were seen. If the hoof prints can be taken as proof of the presence of the animal in this city, there is forcible proof that it has wings, for there is no doubt but what it has gone over high board fences and iron fences, there being no marks to indicate that it stopped to dig its way under. The only thing remaining to verify the presence of this animal is to find some person who will say that they had seen it. Last night citizens who fear that the animal may be a ferocious character went armed and going to their lodges, clubs and other places. The footprints are found about many of the henneries in the upper section of the city, and this is given rise to the belief that the queer thing is a species of fowl.

It was suggested that the odor from the banana oil might have attracted it to the scene of the Chester enamel company's plant, but nothing was missing about the place although the hoof prints would indicate that whatever it is made a thorough inspection of the entire plant and grounds, and particularly about the house containing the compositions used in curing the hides.

It is evidently an animal or creature which has no horror of "ghosts," for the imprints of its hooves are numerous and the Chester rural cemetery.

The same day came this piece from the *Evening Journal* on January 22, 1909. Unfortunately, it's pretty clear that this article is more of an obvious satire as opposed to a serious attempt at a hoax. Several of the scientists quoted in the next two articles are clearly made up, for instance.

HIST! JOBBERWOCK HERE. SPITS FIRE!

Creature Attacks Night Officer, who Says It Screams Like a Lion. Down State Citizens See "It"; Many Alarmed.

The uncanny creature known variously as the "air boss," the "Leeds devil," "Jobbernosk" and the "Grosswauk" that has started all New

Jersey and Pennsylvania has come into Delaware. Last night it was reported to have been seen in Brandywine Village, Elsmere, duPont's Banks, Holly Oak, Hillcrest and Claymont. It is believed the monster came from Philadelphia, where it has been scaring people for several nights.

It was first seen last night at Brandywine Village. Big Policeman Frank Kane was walking along Concord Avenue at midnight when he saw something that looked like an open umbrella squeezed against a fence. His curiosity excited, the portly officer walked forward to examine it more closely when there was a peculiar screech of anger and the object sprang at him. There was but a brief struggle for Officer Kane is one of the strongest men on the force and the creature was being rapidly subdued. Just when it appeared that Kane had the creature under control, however, it gave a wrench, tore from his grasp and disappeared up West street. Mrs. Jane Maguire who lives in the street, says she saw the "devil" pass her door.

The policeman is now recovering from his chilly experience. He is unable to describe the animal accurately, owing to the darkness, but he declares it had blazing green eyes, screeched like a loon and had a pelt like a horse. The creature was as large as a calf he says.

Reports from the suburbs tell of the creature's visit to many places during the night. This morning there were numerous phone calls to THE EVENING JOURNAL announcing that the monstrous thing had been seen in many parts of Brandywine Hundred. Mrs. Smith Jones, of Elsmere, was one of those who excitedly called up THE JOURNAL. The "Thing" had left a single footmark in the snow in front of her front door. This confirms the reports from New Jersey that the creature has but one leg. The footprint is like that of a horse, Mrs. Jones says.

At Holly Oak and Hillcrest, it is reported that during the night the "devil" devoured several garbage cans. It also has a tooth for front doorsteps, chickens, dogs, ash barrels, tool chests and beer and coffee, according to many who have suffered by its ravages.

Dr. Mynhaur Beeskobe, Belgian scientist, who is visiting friends in the city, was interviewed by an EVENING JOURNAL reporter this morning concerning the freak. The doctor very kindly left a very large dinner of sauerkraut and wurst to talk to the reporter. It is his belief that the unknown creature is a relic of a very rare specimen of the Cos Ingeniorum and is closely related to the Copia Verborum, which although practically extinct, is found occasionally in his own country.

"If the papeer will but bring me zee animal I weel tell you more. It woel be veer, veer simple," he said.

THE EVENING JOURNAL has dispatched its office boy to Brandywine hundred in search of the beast. He is armed with a huge net and a squirt gun. The boy will appreciate the assistance of public-spirited citizens in his efforts to corral the bug.

Dr. Albert Robin gives no credence to a suggested theory that the mysterious animal-bird is a Brandywine water bacteria that has fled because of a fear of being corralled in the proposed new filter, nor does he think it one of the microbes lie says were walking in an alley near Twelfth street recently.

LEFT TRACKS LIKE A PONY.

The creature must have paid a visit to the rear yard of the home of S.S. Harris, at No. 8 West Nineteenth street on Wednesday night. Its footprints were found in the yard yesterday morning. Mr. Harris and his son came to the conclusion that a Shetland pony had been in the yard. The prints in the snow were just like those which would be made by a horse.

The tracks of the animal lead from one end of the yard to the other and it must have crawled under the fence for there is no evidence of it having jumped over it. The tracks lead on beyond the fence, but the Harris' did not follow them.

PTERNADON! SO SAYS PROFESSOR BUGG.

Special to THE EVENING JOURNAL.
NEWARK, Jan. 22. - Professor Harry Hayward of the Agricultural Experimental

Stations was away today and his views as to the Leeds Devil could not be obtained. Professor Hayward, it was stated, had gone to Pennsylvania, but officials at the experimental station denied that he was searching for the "Jobberwock."

Professor Bugg, an authority of this town, consented to talk of the strange bird-animal. "In my opinion it is a pternadon," he said. "You know the pternadon was a strange creature of the air that figured in mythology. Who knows but that this prehistoric creature has not become reality? I have grave fears for the safety of our citizens if this should be so, for the pternadon was a monster vampire, with feet of peculiar formation. No other animal or beast had such feet, and it always left a trail that could be traced readily, only to end in nothingness, for the pternadon could fly even more rapidly than it could traverse the earth. So speedy was its flight that the sound of the terrible whirr of its wings was followed in an instant by an attack, and with one blow of its sword-like beak and a ripping with its talons its victim was left lifeless, mangled, torn worse than by an bloodthirsty cannibal. I hardly credit, though, that the pternadon has become a reality, even in this day of startling things."

MAY USE AIR SHOVEL AS CANAL DIGGER.

Special to THE EVENING JOURNAL.

LEWES, Del., Jan. 22. - Congressman Hiram R. Burton is much interested in the stories of the peregrinations of the Leeds Devil about Philadelphia. He hopes the singular monster of air and land will develop the qualities of uprooting the earth, and if it does, he is in favor of raising many of the animals for use in digging out the Chesapeake and Delaware Canal.

MILFORD NOT SEEING THINGS.

MILFORD. Del., Jan. 22. - Colonel Theodore Townsend says no apparition like the Leeds Devil has been seen about Milford. "Folks down here don't see such things" said the Colonel. "You know Milford is now 'dry' and there is not the inspiration to see things." Colonel Townsend says he had heard of no movement to call out Company B of the militia to guard against a visitation of the air-devil.

WHAT THE DEVIL? LOOKS LIKE HIM.

New Britain Herald- July 3,1924 - Connecticut West Orange, N.J., Reports Strange Monster. New York, July 3. - The lieutenant in charge of the West Orange, N.J., police station answered the telephone yesterday afternoon and found that Patrolman George Deckenback and a lot of excitement were on the wire, "Say!" said the policeman. "Say, I just seen something!"
The lieutenant immediately motioned to the three policemen on reserve, and they piled into the station house automobile and went roaring

away to Patrolman Deckenback's post, while the policeman continued:

"I just seen an animal that has a head like a deer, that runs like a rabbit and has fiery eyes. What do you think it is?"

The lieutenant talked as soothingly as possible, meanwhile writing a note to another policeman to bring Chief Patrick Donough. By the time the chief arrived the three reserves came back with Patrolman Deckenback sitting with them in their automobile. Deckenback launched into a description of the strange animal he had seen, while the others patted him on the back and told him not to worry. Deckenback was beginning to think they weren't believing him, when Mrs. Clyde Vincent, of Pleasant Valley, came breathlessly into the station with her two children.

"Lieutenant," she said finally, "we were picnicking on the road a while ago when an animal that had a head like a deer, ran like a rabbit and had fiery eyes came along and jumped over us."

Latter Patrolman Deckenback received further vindication when Chief James Ashby, of the Livingston police, telephoned that a farmer there had reported seeing the "devil" jumping about his fields. Several policemen and fifty' boys passed the rest of the afternoon searching for the creature, but unsuccessfully.

The West Orange police think the animal is a kangaroo that escaped from a circus or zoo, though they are stumped by the fiery eyes.

INDEX

Arch Street Museum, 155

Arment, Chad, 19, 25

baby dinosaurs, 21-24, 117, 242

Baca, Juan, 225, 228

Bateman, Bramblett, 266, 268, 272, 276

Big Bend, 89, 110, 117, 118

Bigfoot, 14, 185, 195, 216, 312

Billy the Kid, 244, 312

Bishop's Cap, 245, 248, 253

Bladenboro Beast, 18, 56-82

Boaz Mastodon, 234-236

Boaz, Wisconsin, 233-237

Boonville Monster, 190

Boyer, Dennis, 233, 235, 238

Bryant, Patricia, 103-106

Bunnell, Charles E., 126-128

Canyon Lake Gorge, 239-240

Carlsbad Caverns, 157

Carrizozo, New Mexico, 226

Childress, David Hatcher, 294

Churubusco, Indiana, 170-185

Cohen, Daniel, 156, 175, 185

Coleman, Loren, 130, 203

Colorado River Dinos, 19-25, 113

Conan Doyle, Sir Arthur, 12, 119, 284

Conkling, Roscoe, 246-249

Conrad, Frank D., 161

Crosswicks Monster, 18, 208-209

Cryptopia, 107-108, 128, 133

Cullen, Terry, 197-198

Cyprinodon diabolis, 286

Death Valley, 283-294

Devil's Hole, 286-287, 293-294

Dinsdale, Tim, 15

Dog Eater, 18, 57-59, 66

Dragon of Death Valley, 285-286

Eohippus, 283

Flatwoods Monster, 17

Fores, Chief Roy, 62-72

Fort, Charles, 130

Fountain, Albert J., 243-244

Fulk, Oscar, 172-173,

Gerhard, Ken, 109-110

giant rattlesnakes, 222-232

Gimlin, Bob, 15-16

Glacier Island Monster, 122-134

Golden Age of Newspapers, 12

Golden Age of UFOs, 14

Gonzales, Mike, 224, 228

Grant, Arthur, 14, 52

Grimaldo, Armando, 94, 97-98

Guadalupe Mountains, 228

Guajardo, Alverco, 94, 97

Hall, Mark A., 209

Hansen, Frank D., 197-202

Harris, Gail, 172-183, 303

Heuvelmans, Bernard, 14-15, 198, 200-201, 203-204

Hopkins, T.F., 155

Hopper Whoppers, 161-162

Houdini, Harry, 12

Jameson, W.C., 230, 232, 261-264

Jeffries, Norman, 155, 156

Jersey Devil, 138-156, 214, 221, 295-306

Keel, John, 117, 194-195

Lake Campbell, South Dakota, 49, 51-52, 54

Lake Elsinore, California, 254-258

Lake Walgren, Nebraska, 28-48

Las Gallinas Creek Monster, 258-260

Lawson, Douglas, 92, 110

Loch Ness Monster, 13, 52, 54, 242, 255, 258

Lost World, The (1925), 11

Mackal, Dr. Roy P., 281

Maher, John G., 45

Manson, Charles, 293-294

McDonald, W.J., 125, 127-129

mermaids, 29, 32, 45, 47-48, 279

Milton Monster, 18, 205-210

Minnesota Ice Man, 196-204

Mountain Boomer, 117

Neomylodon, 187, 249

Nessie, 14-15, 52, 242, 255-257

O'Brien, Willis, 12

Oscar, the turtle, 170-185

Paiute tribe, 288-289

Patterson, Roger, 15-16

petrified caveman, 26

Piasa Bird, 263

Pine Barrens, New Jersey, 140

Quetzalcoatlus northropi, 110

Resendez, Alex, 107-108

Roosevelt, Theodore, 216

Sanderson, Ivan T., 14, 198-200, 203

Scahffer, Ron, 19

Shuker, Karl, 130, 133

skinwalker, 81

Smithsonian Institute, 202, 216

Snaik Stories, 12, 16, 18

Snake People, 228-231

Snallygaster, 212-221

Snow, Myrtle, 21-23

Society of American Magicians, 12

Sucik, Nick, 19-25, 113, 115-118

Surgeon's Photo, 13, 15-16, 54

Texas "Big Bird", 18, 88-111, 139

Tombstone Thunderbird, 13-14, 23, 90, 168

Trunko, 129, 133

Turtle Days Festival, 184

Valley of Fires, 223

Valley of Gwangi, The, 283

Vevig, Tom, 130-131

War of the Worlds, 10-11

Warren, Cloyce, 280, 282

Westring, Helen, 201-202

White River Monster, 265-282

White Sands, New Mexico, 243-253

Wingate Pass,
    California, 288-289,
    293

Wright, Ellis, 84, 87,
    250-252

ARTIST CONCEPTS

ABOUT THE AUTHOR

John LeMay was born and raised in Roswell, NM, the "UFO Capital of the World." He is the author of over 40 books on film and western history such as *Kong Unmade: The Lost Films of Skull Island, Tall Tales and Half Truths of Billy the Kid,* and *Roswell USA: Towns That Celebrate UFOs, Lake Monsters, Bigfoot and Other Weirdness.* In addition to non-fiction, he is also the author of the novel *The Noted Desperado Pancho Dumez.* He is also the editor/publisher of *The Lost Films Fanzine, Strange West Magazine* and has written for magazines such as *True West, Cinema Retro,* and *Mad Scientist* to name only a few. He is a Past President of the Board of Directors for the Historical Society for Southeast New Mexico and the host of the web series *Roswell's Hidden History.*

THE BICEP BOOKS CATALOGUE

The following titles are available for purchase on Amazon.com, and are available to bookstores at a wholesale discount via Ingram Content Group (ISBNs of available editions listed for this purpose)

THE BIG BOOK OF JAPANESE GIANT MONSTER MOVIES SERIES

The third edition of the book that started it all! Reviews over 100 tokusatsu films between 1954 and 1988. All the Godzilla, Gamera, and Daimajin movies made during the Showa era are covered plus lesser known fare like *Invisible Man vs. The Human Fly* (1957) and *Conflagration* (1975). Softcover (380 pp/5.83" X 8.27") Suggested Retail: $19.99 SBN:978-1-7341546-4-1

This third edition reviews over 75 tokusatsu films between 1989 and 2019. All the Godzilla, Gamera, and Ultraman movies made during the Heisei era are covered plus independent films like *Reigo, King of the Sea Monsters* (2005), *Demeking, the Sea Monster* (2009) and *Attack of the Giant Teacher* (2019)! Softcover (260 pp/5.83" X 8.27") Suggested Retail: $19.99 ISBN: 978-1- 7347816-4-9

This second edition of the Rondo Award nominated book covers un-produced scripts like *Bride of Godzilla* (1955), partially shot movies like *Giant Horde Beast Nezura* (1963), and banned films like *Prophecies of Nostradamus* (1974), plus hundreds of other lost productions. Softcover/Hard-cover (470pp. /7" X 10") Suggested Retail: $24.99 (sc)/$39.95(hc)ISBN: 978-1-73 41546-0-3 (hc)

This sequel to *The Lost Films* covers the non-giant monster unmade movie scripts from Japan such as *Frankenstein vs. the Human Vapor* (1963), *After Japan Sinks* (1974-76), plus lost movies like *Fearful Attack of the Flying Saucers* (1956) and *Venus Flytrap* (1968). Hardcover (200 pp/5.03" X 8.27")/Softcover (216 pp/ 5.5" X 8.5") Suggested Retail: $9.99 (sc)/$24.99(hc) ISBN:978-1-7341546 -3-4 (hc)

This companion book to *The Lost Films* charts the development of all the prominent Japanese monster movies including discarded screenplays, story ideas, and deleted scenes. Also includes bios for writers like Shinichi Sekizawa, Niisan Takahashi and many others. Comprehensive script listing and appendices as well. Hardcover/Softcover (370 pp./ 6"X9") Suggested Retail: $16.95(sc)/$34.99(hc)ISBN: 978-1-7341546-5-8 (hc)

Examines the differences between the U.S. and Japanese versions of over 50 different tokusatsu films like *Gojira* (1954)/*Godzilla, King of the Monsters!* (1956), *Gamera* (1965)/*Gammera, the Invincible* (1966), *Submersion of Japan* (1973)/*Tidal Wave* (1975), and many, many more! Softcover (540 pp./ 6"X9") Suggested Retail: $22.99 ISBN: 978-1-953221-77 -3

Examines the differences between the European and Japanese versions of tokusatsu films including the infamous "Cozzilla" colorized version of *Godzilla*, from 1977, plus rarities like *Terremoto 10 Grado*, the Italian cut of *Legend of Dinosaurs*. The book also examines the condensed Champion Matsuri edits of Toho's effects films. Softcover (372 pp./ 6"X9") Suggested Retail: $19.99 ISBN: 978-1- 953221-77-3

Throughout the 1960s and 1970s the Italian film industry cranked out over 600 "Spaghetti Westerns" and for every *Fistful of Dollars* were a dozen pale imitations, some of them hilarious. Many of these lesser known Spaghettis are available in bargain bin DVD packs and for free online. If ever you've wondered which are worth your time and which aren't, this is the book for you. Softcover (160pp./5.06" X 7.8") Suggested Retail: $9.99

THE BICEP BOOKS CATALOGUE

CLASSIC MONSTERS SERIES

Kong Unmade explores unproduced scripts like *King Kong vs. Frankenstein* (1958), unfinished films like *The Lost Island* (1934), and lost movies like *King Kong Appears in Edo* (1938). As a bonus, all the Kong rip-offs like *Konga* (1961) and *Queen Kong* (1976) are reviewed. Hardcover (350 pp/5.83" X 8.27")/Softcover (376 pp/ 5.5" X 8.5") Suggested Retail: $24.99 (hc)/$19.99(sc) ISBN: 978-1-7341546-2-7(hc)

Jaws Unmade explores unproduced scripts like *Jaws 3, People 0* (1979), abandoned ideas like a Quint prequel, and even aborted sequels to *Jaws Part II*. As a bonus, all the Jaws rip-offs like *Grizzly* (1976) and *Tentacles* (1977) are reviewed. Hardcover (316 pp/5.83" X 8.27")/Softcover (340 pp/5.5" X 8.5") Suggested Retail: $29.99 (hc)/$17.95(sc) ISBN: 978-1-7344730-1-8

Classic Monsters Unmade covers lost and unmade films starring Dracula, Frankenstein, the Mummy and more monsters. Reviews unmade scripts like *The Return of Frankenstein* (1934) and *Wolf Man vs. Dracula* (1944). It also examines lost films of the silent era such as *The Werewolf* (1913) and *Drakula's Death* (1923). Softcover/ Hardcover(428pp/5.83"X8.27") Suggested Retail: $22.99(sc)/ $27.99(hc)ISBN:978-1-953221-85-8(hc)

Volume 2 explores the Hammer era and beyond, from unmade versions of *Brides of Dracula* (called *Disciple of Dracula*) to remakes of *Creature from the Black Lagoon*. Completely unmade films like *Kali: Devil Bride of Dracula* (1975) and *Godzilla vs. Frankenstein* (1964) are covered along with lost completed films like *Batman Fights Dracula* (1967) and *Black the Ripper* (1974). Coming Fall 2021.

NOSTALGIA

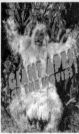

Written in the same spirit as *The Big Book of Japanese Giant Monster Movies*, this tome reviews all the classic Universal and Hammer horrors to star Dracula, Frankenstein, the Gillman and the rest along with obscure flicks like *The New Invisible Man* (1958), *Billy the Kid versus Dracula* (1966), *Blackenstein* (1973) and *Legend of the Werewolf* (1974). Softcover (394 pp/5.5" X 8.5") Suggested Retail: $17.95

Written at an intermediate reading level for the kid in all of us, these picture books will take you back to your youth. In the spirit of the old Ian Thorne books are covered *Nabonga* (1944), *White Pongo* (1945) and more! Hardcover/Softcover (44 pp/7.5" X 9.25") Suggested Retail: $17.95(hc)/$9.99(sc) ISBN: 978- 1-7341546-9-6 (hc) 978- 1-7344730-5-6 (sc)

Written at an intermediate reading level for the kid in all of us, these picture books will take you back to your youth. In the spirit of the old Ian Thorne books are covered *The Lost World* (1925), *The Land That Time Forgot* (1975) and more! Hardcover/Softcover (44 pp/7.5" X 9.25") Suggested Retail: $17.95 (hc)/$9.99(sc) ISBN: 978-1-7344730 -6-3 (hc) 978- 1-7344730-7-0 (sc)

Written at an intermediate reading level for the kid in all of us, these picture books will take you back to your youth. In the spirit of the old Ian Thorne books are covered *Them!* (1954), *Empire of the Ants* (1977) and more! Hardcover/ Softcover (44 pp/7.5" X 9.25") Suggested Retail: $17.95(hc)/ $9.99(sc) ISBN: 978-1-7347816 -3-2 (hc) 978 -1-7347816-2-5 (sc)

THE BICEP BOOKS CATALOGUE

CRYPTOZOOLOGY/COWBOYS & SAURIANS

Cowboys & Saurians: Prehistoric Beasts as Seen by the Pioneers explores dinosaur sightings from the pioneer period via real newspaper reports from the time. Well-known cases like the Tombstone Thunderbird are covered along with more obscure cases like the Crosswicks Monster and more. Softcover (357 pp/5.06" X 7.8") Suggested Retail: $19.95 ISBN: 978-1-7341546-1-0

Cowboys & Saurians: Ice Age zeroes in on snowbound saurians like the Cerato-saurus of the Arctic Circle and a Tyrannosaurus of the Tundra, as well as sightings of Ice Age megafauna like mammoths, glyptodonts, Sarkastodons and Saber-toothed tigers. Tales of a land that time forgot in the Arctic are also covered. Softcover (264 pp/5.06" X 7.8") Suggested Retail: $14.99 ISBN: 978-1-7341546-7-2

Southerners & Saurians takes the series formula of exploring newspaper accounts of monsters in the pioneer period with an eye to the Old South. In addition to dinosaurs are covered Lizardmen, Frogmen, giant leeches and mosquitoes, and the Dingocroc, which might be an alien rather than a prehistoric survivor. Softcover (202 pp/5.06" X 7.8") Suggested Retail: $13.99 ISBN: 978-1-7344730-4-9

Cowboys & Saurians South of the Border explores the saurians of Central and South America, like the Patagonian Plesiosaurus that was really an Iemisch, plus tales of the Neo-Mylodon, a menacing monster from underground called the Minhocao, Glyptodonts, and even Bolivia's three-headed dinosaur! Softcover (412 pp/ 5.06"X7.8") Suggested Retail: $17.95 ISBN: 978-1-953221-73-5

UFOLOGY/THE REAL COWBOYS & ALIENS IN CONJUNCTION WITH ROSWELL BOOKS

The Real Cowboys and Aliens: Early American UFOs explores UFO sightings in the USA between the years 1800-1864. Stories of encounters sometimes involved famous figures in U.S. history such as Lewis and Clark, and Thomas Jefferson.Hardcover (242pp/6" X 9") Softcover (262 pp/5.06" X 7.8") Suggested Retail: $24.99 (hc)/$15.95(sc) ISBN: 978-1-7341546-8-9\(hc)/978-1-7344730-8-7(sc)

The second entry in the series, *Old West UFOs*, covers reports spanning the years 1865-1895. Includes tales of Men in Black, Reptilians, Spring-Heeled Jack, Sasquatch from space, and other alien beings, in addition to the UFOs and airships. Hardcover (276 pp/6" X 9") Softcover (308 pp/5.06" X 7.8") Suggested Retail: $29.95 (hc)/$17.95(sc) ISBN: 978-1-7344730-0-1 (hc)/ 978-1-7344730-2-5 (sc)

The third entry in the series, *The Coming of the Airships*, encompasses a short time frame with an incredibly high concentration of airship sightings between 1896-1899. The famous Aurora, Texas, UFO crash of 1897 is covered in depth along with many others. Hardcover (196 pp/6" X 9") Softcover (222 pp/5.06" X 7.8") Suggested Retail: $24.99 (hc)/$15.95(sc) ISBN: 978-1-7347816 -1-8 (hc)/978-1-7347816-0-1(sc)

Early 20th Century UFOs: American Sightings kicks off a new series that investigates UFO sightings of the early 1900s. Includes tales of UFOs sighted over the Titanic as it sunk, Nikola Tesla receiving messages from the stars, an alien being found encased in ice, and a possible virus from outer space!Hardcover (196 pp/6" X 9") Softcover (222 pp/5.06" X 7.8") Suggested Retail: $27.99 (hc)/$16.95(sc) ISBN: 978-1-7347816-1-8 (hc)/978-1-73478 16-0-1(sc)

LOST FILMS FANZINE BACK ISSUES

THE LOST FILMS FANZINE VOL.1

ISSUE #1 SPRING 2020 The lost Italian cut of *Legend of Dinosaurs and Monster Birds* called *Terremoto 10 Grado*, plus *Bride of Dr. Phibes* script, *Good Luck! Godzilla*, the King Kong remake that became a car commercial, Bollywood's lost *Jaws* rip-off, Top Ten Best Fan Made Godzilla trailers plus an interview with Scott David Lister. 60 pages. Three variant covers/editions (premium color/basic color/ b&w)

ISSUE #2 SUMMER 2020 How 1935's *The Capture of Tarzan* became 1936's *Tarzan Escapes*, the Orca sequels that weren't, Baragon in Bollywood's *One Million B.C.*, unmade *Kolchak: The Night Stalker* movies, *The Norliss Tapes*, *Superman V: The New Movie*, why there were no *Curse of the Pink Panther* sequels, *Moonlight Mask: The Movie*. 64 pages. Two covers/ editions (basic color/b&w)

ISSUE #3 FALL 2020 Blob sequels both forgotten and unproduced, *Horror of Dracula* uncut, *Frankenstein Meets the Wolfman* and talks, myths of the lost *King Kong* Spider-Pit sequence debunked, the *Carnosaur* novel vs. the movies, *Terror in the Streets* 50th anniversary, *Bride of Godzilla* 55th Unniversary, Lee Powers sketchbook. 100 pages. Two covers/editions (basic color/b&w)

ISSUE #4 WINTER 2020/21 *Diamonds Are Forever's* first draft with Goldfinger, *Disciple of Dracula* into *Brides of Dracula*, *War of the Worlds That Weren't* Part II, *Day the Earth Stood Still II* by Ray Bradbury, *Deathwish 6*, *Atomic War Bride*, *What Am I Doing in the Middle of a Revolution?*, *Spring Dream in the Old Capital* and more. 70 pages. Two covers/editions (basic color/b&w)

THE LOST FILMS FANZINE VOL.2

ISSUE #5 SPRING 2021 The lost films and projects of ape suit performer Charles Gemora, plus *Superman Reborn*, *Teenage Mutant Ninja Turtles IV: The Next Mutation*, *Mikado Zombie*, NBC's *Big Stuffed Dog*, King Ghidorah flies solo, *Grizzly H* reviewed, and War of the Worlds That Weren't concludes with a musical. Plus Blu-Ray reviews, news, and letters. 66 pages. Two covers/editions (basic color/ b&w)

ISSUE #6 SUMMER 2021 Peter Sellers *Romance of the Pink Panther*, Akira Kurosawa's *Song of the Horse*, *Kali - Devil Bride of Dracula*, Jack Black as Green Lantern, *Ladybug, Ladybug*, *The Lost Atlantis*, Japan's lost superhero Hiyo Man, and *Lord of Light*, the CIA's covert movie that inspired 2012's *Argo*. Plus news, Blu-Ray reviews, news, and letters. 72 pages. Two covers/editions (basic color/b&w)

ISSUE #7 FALL 2021 *Hiero's Journey*, Don Bragg in *Tarzan and the Jewels of Opar*, DC's *Lobo* movie, Lee Powers Scrapbook returns, Blake Matthews uncovers *The Big Boss Part II* (1976), Matthew B. Lamont searches for lost Three Stooges, and an ape called Kong in 1927's *Isle of Sunken Gold*. Plus news, and letters. 72 pages. Two covers/editions (basic color /b&w)

ISSUE #8 WINTER 2021/22 The connection between Steve Reeves' unmade third Hercules movie and *Goliath and the Dragon*, *The Iron Man* starring Tom Cruise, Phil Yordan's *King Kong* remake, *The Unearthly Stranger*, *Saturday Supercade* forgotten cartoon, the 45th anniversary of Luigi Cozzi's "Cozzilla" and *Day the Earth Froze*. Plus news and letters. 72 pages. Two covers/editions (basic color /b&w)

MOVIE MILESTONES BACK ISSUES

MOVIE MILESTONES VOL. 1   VOL. 2

ISSUE #1 AUGUST 2020 Debut issue celebrating 80 years of *One Million B.C.* (1940), and an early 55th Anniversary for *One Million Years B.C.* (1966). Abandoned ideas, casting changes, and deleted scenes are covered, plus, a mini-B.C. stock-footage filmography and much more! 54 pages. Three collectible covers/editions (premium color/basic color/b&w)

ISSUE #2 OCTOBER 2020 Celebrates the joint 50th Anniversaries of *When Dinosaurs Ruled the Earth* (1970) and *Creatures the World Forgot* (1971). Also includes looks at *Prehistoric Women* (1967), *When Women Had Tails* (1970), and *Caveman* (1981), plus unmade films like *When the World Cracked Open*. 72 pages. Three collectible covers/editions (premium color/basic color/b&w)

ISSUE #3 WINTER 2021 Japanese 'Panic Movies' like *The Last War* (1961), *Submersion of Japan* (1973), and *Bullet Train* (1975) are covered on celebrated author Sakyo Komatsu's 90th birthday. The famous banned Toho film *Prophecies of Nostradamus* (1974) are also covered. 124 pages. Three collectible covers/editions (premium color/ basic color/ b&w)

ISSUE #4 SPRING 2021 This issue celebrates the joint 60th Anniversaries of *Gorgo, Reptilicus* and *Konga* examining unmade sequels like *Reptilicus 2*, and other related lost projects like *Kuru Island* and *The Volcano Monsters*. Also explores the Gorgo, Konga and Reptilicus comic books from Charlton. 72 pages. Three collectible covers/editions (premium color/basic color/b&w)

MOVIE MILESTONES VOL. 2   VOL. 3 COMING SOON

ISSUE #5 SUMMER 2021 *Godzilla vs. the Sea Monster* gets the spotlight, with an emphasis on its original version *King Kong vs. Ebirah*, plus information on *The King Kong Show* which inspired it, and Jun Fukuda's tangentially related spy series *100 Shot/100 Killed*. 72 pages. Three collectible covers/editions (premium color /basic color/b&w)

ISSUE #6 FALL 2021 Monster Westerns of the 1950s and 1960s are spotlighted in the form of *Teenage Monster, The Curse of the Undead, Billy the Kid Versus Dracula, Jesse James Meets Frankenstein's Daughter,* and Bela Lugosi's unmade *The Ghoul Goes West*. 50 pages. Special Black and White exclusive!

ISSUE #7 WINTER 2022 This issue is all about Amicus's Edgar Rice Burroughs trilogy including *Land That Time Forgot, At the Earth's Core, People That Time Forgot* plus unmade sequels like *Out of Time's Abyss* or Doug McClure as John Carter of Mars. All this plus *Warlords of Atlantis* and *Arabian Adventure*! 100 pages. Three collectible covers/editions (premium color /basic color/b&w)

ISSUE #8 SPRING 2022 *Godzilla vs. Gigan* turns 50 and this issue is here to celebrate with its many unmade versions, like *Godzilla vs. the Space Monsters* and *Return of King Ghidorah,* plus *The Mysterians* 65th anniversary and *Daigoro vs. Goliath's* 50th.

NEW RELEASES

DON'T MISS THE SUPPLEMENTARY MAGAZINE!

Printed in Great Britain
by Amazon

34593110R00176